BOOK TWO

The Take-Action Guide to
World Class
Learners

*This book is dedicated to helping schools and teachers
to transform their educational setting into a global campus so as
to enable the development of globally competent entrepreneurs.*

BOOK TWO

The Take-Action Guide to
World Class
Learners

How to "Make" Product-Oriented
Learning Happen

Yong Zhao

Homa Tavangar • Emily McCarren •
Gabriel F. Rshaid • Kay Tucker

CORWIN
A SAGE Publishing Company

A SAGE Publishing Company

FOR INFORMATION:

Corwin

A SAGE Company

2455 Teller Road

Thousand Oaks, California 91320

(800) 233-9936

www.corwin.com

SAGE Publications Ltd.

1 Oliver's Yard

55 City Road

London EC1Y 1SP

United Kingdom

SAGE Publications India Pvt. Ltd.

B 1/I 1 Mohan Cooperative Industrial Area

Mathura Road, New Delhi 110 044

India

SAGE Publications Asia-Pacific Pte. Ltd.

3 Church Street

#10-04 Samsung Hub

Singapore 049483

Executive Editor: Arnis Burvikovs

Associate Editor: Desirée A. Bartlett

Editorial Assistant: Andrew Olson

Production Editor: Amy Schroller

Copy Editor: Lana Arndt

Typesetter: C&M Digitals (P) Ltd.

Proofreader: Laura Webb

Indexer: Rick Hurd

Cover Designer: Rose Storey

Marketing Manager: Kimberly Kanakes

Printed in the United States of America

Library of Congress Cataloging-in-Publication Data

Names: Zhao, Yong, 1965- author.

Title: The take-action guide to world class learners. Book 2, How to "make" product-oriented learning happen / Zong Zhao, Homa Tavangar, Emily McCarren, Gabriel F. Rshaid, Kay Tucker.

Other titles: How to "make" product-oriented learning happen

Description: Thousand Oaks, Calif. : Corwin, A SAGE Company, 2016. | Includes index.

Identifiers: LCCN 2015040123 | ISBN 978-1-4833-3951-1 (pbk.: alk. paper)

Subjects: LCSH: Project method in teaching. | Entrepreneurship–Study and teaching–Activity programs. | Education and globalization.

Classification: LCC LB1027.43 .Z53 2016 | DDC 371.3/6–dc23 LC record available at http://lccn.loc.gov/2015040123

Certified Chain of Custody
Promoting Sustainable Forestry
www.sfiprogram.org
SFI-01268

SFI label applies to text stock

16 17 18 19 20 10 9 8 7 6 5 4 3 2 1

Contents

About the Authors

Yong Zhao currently serves as the presidential chair and director of the Institute for Global and Online Education in the College of Education, University of Oregon, where he is also a professor in the Department of Educational Measurement, Policy, and Leadership. He is also a professorial fellow at the Mitchell Institute for Health and Education Policy, Victoria University. His works focus on the implications of globalization and technology on education. He has published over 100 articles and 20 books, including *Who's Afraid of the Big Bad Dragon: Why China has the Best (and Worst) Education System in the World, Catching Up or Leading the Way: American Education in the Age of Globalization* and *World Class Learners: Educating Creative and Entrepreneurial Students*. He is a recipient of the Early Career Award from the American Educational Research Association and was named one of the 2012 ten most influential people in educational technology by the *Tech & Learn Magazine*. He is an elected fellow of the International Academy for Education. His latest book *World Class Learners* has won several awards including the Society of Professors of Education Book Award (2013), Association of Education Publishers' (AEP) Judges' Award and Distinguished Achievement Award in Education Leadership (2013).

Homa Sabet Tavangar is the author of *Growing Up Global: Raising Children to Be At Home in the World* and *The Global Education Toolkit for Elementary Learners*, and contributor to *Mastering Global Literacy* by Heidi Hayes-Jacobs. Homa's work is sparking initiatives to help audiences from CEOs to kindergartners learn and thrive in a global context—and have fun along the way. She is an education and cultural consultant to NBC TV on original programming; she is also a contributing writer for the *Huffington Post*, PBS, Momsrising, GOOD, Ashoka's Start Empathy, *National Geographic*, and Edutopia, among other media, and is a sought-after speaker and trainer around globalization and global citizenship, parenting, globalizing curriculum, empathy, diversity, and inclusion. Homa spent 20 years working in global competitiveness, organizational, business, and international development with hundreds of businesses, nonprofits, and public organizations, before turning her attention to global education. She speaks four languages, and her religious heritage includes four of the world's major faiths. Passionate around issues of opportunity and equality for women and girls, she has worked on these issues for private companies and the World Bank, and served on various nonprofit boards including currently on the Board and Executive Committee of the Tahirih Justice Center, a national leader protecting immigrant women and girls fleeing violence. She is married and the mother of three daughters.

Emily McCarren is the high school principal at the Punahou School in Honolulu, Hawaii, the largest single campus K–12 independent school in the United States. Originally from Vermont, McCarren graduated from Colby College in Maine where she majored in Spanish and biology, and was a two-sport athlete, captaining the alpine ski team and lacrosse team. She holds two master's degrees: in Spanish Literature from the Saint Louis University's Madrid campus and in Educational Leadership from the Klingenstein Center at Teachers College, Columbia University. She is completing her Ph.D. in educational technology at the University of Hawaii, where her dissertation examines the role of teacher care on a student's online learning experience. McCarren began her career teaching Spanish and geometry at Swiss Semester, a program for American students in the Swiss Alps. Next, she worked at The Thacher School in Ojai, California, where she taught, coached, and served as a residential advisor for 6 years before joining the faculty at the Punahou School in Honolulu, Hawaii, in 2006. At Punahou, she has taught all levels of Academy Spanish and a year of biology, served as a department head of both Asian-Pacific and European Languages, and as Academy Summer School director. McCarren was appointed to lead Punahou's Wo International Center in 2012, where she worked to broaden the global perspective of students and faculty while strengthening Punahou's role as a global educational leader.

Gabriel F. Rshaid is the headmaster of St. Andrew's Scots School in Buenos Aires, Argentina, the oldest bilingual school in the world, and a Professional Development Associate with the Leadership and Learning Center in Denver, Colorado. A former board member of ASCD, he is the author of the following books: *Learning for the Future: Rethinking Schools for the 21st Century*, *The 21st Century Classroom*, and *From Out of This World: Leadership and Life Lessons From the Space Program*. He has presented all over the world on the future of learning and 21st Century Education, as well as conducted numerous workshops, retreats, and seminars for educators and administrators.

 **Kay Tucker's** vision and passion is to actively engage in defining and creating a culture for World Class Learning. She collaborates with educators to create ecosystems for sustainable learning including space, context, and technologies; designs and implements professional development opportunities; and originates systems and tools to impact change. As the World Class Education Specialist at Lone Tree Elementary in Douglas County Colorado, she is in charge of creating a model of teaching and learning driven by current global educational reform and a World Class Education based on the thinking of Dr. Yong Zhao. In this model, students learn in an integrated manner as they align their strengths and passions in solving problems within a real-world context. In flexible environments, students navigate curriculum through inquiry and create their own learning pathways, while teachers facilitate opportunities, provide resources, and target teach on an as-needed basis. Kay Tucker's career in education spans 20 years. She has an undergraduate degree in fine arts from the University of Colorado Boulder and a master's degree in curriculum and instruction from the University of Colorado at Denver.

Introduction

Making World Class Learners

by Yong Zhao

No More Boomerang Kids

"One in five people in their 20s and early 30s is currently living with his or her parents," writes a 2014 *New York Times Magazine* article, "and 60 percent of all young adults receive financial support from them. That's a significant increase from a generation ago, when only one in 10 young adults moved back home and few received financial support." The article "It's Official: The Boomerang Kids Won't Leave" once again brought much attention to the issue of the economic conditions of today's youth, the boomerang generation. For many reasons, mostly the lack of financial resources to be independent, an increasing number of today's youth return to live with their parents, after briefly living away, mostly for pursuing higher education.

Gavin Newton Tanzer

There are of course exceptions. Gavin Newton Tanzer is one of them. Not only is he not returning to live with his parents, but he has been helping others to find hope and future in distant lands. A 25-year-old American living in China, Gavin has founded several companies and nonprofit organizations that help future youth become financially independent and socially responsible individuals in the globalized world. In 2010, while still a student at Columbia University, Gavin founded China Pathway, a company that provides consulting services for Chinese students intending to study abroad and Chinese educational institutions to develop study abroad pathway programs. In 2011, he founded Uexcel International Academy, with Compass Education Group, to bring international school programs to public schools in China. Both businesses have been profitable. He has dabbled in other businesses as well, including founding a company for data mining and even a company for movie production. "Neither of which went anywhere, but stemmed from what I saw as opportunities," said Gavin.

Gavin left home upon graduating from Newtown High School in 2007 at the age of 18. He spent a year in China, learning the language and culture, making friends, and honing his organizational skills by serving at the youth volunteer programs in the 2008 Beijing Olympic Games. He now speaks fluent Mandarin Chinese, with a Beijing accent, in addition to French and Spanish. More importantly, he spotted the need for a better understanding about China. When he returned to attend college at Columbia, he started the Global China Connection (GCC) student organization, which now boasts more than 60 chapters in over 10 countries. GCC connects thousands of future youth leaders who have a desire and are willing to have a better understanding of China and opportunities in China.

But most impressive is Gavin's new venture, which is transforming education in China. In 2012, he founded Sunrise International Education, a company that develops and provides extracurricular programs in China and ultimately globally. The premier program of Sunrise is the introduction of American-style high school debate in China. After only 2 years, Sunrise programs have trained nearly 100,000 Chinese students and organized tournaments with over 6,000 participants. "We are set to have around 12,000 in tournament this year [2014]," according to Gavin. And Sunrise is working on adding two more leagues: drama and business. In many ways, Gavin's programs are delivering more impact on Chinese students than many government reform efforts in terms of helping them develop critical thinking skills, communication and public speaking skills, and independent thinking skills, in addition to broadening their educational experiences. By the way, Gavin's company has over 20 employees, expecting to double that soon.

THE ENTREPRENEURIAL MINDSET

What makes Gavin different from the boomerang kids? The mindset. Gavin has an entrepreneurial mindset that makes him a creator of opportunities and jobs for himself and others. The boomerang kids have the employee mindset that makes them look for jobs that no longer exist. Technology and globalization have transformed our society. Machines and off-shoring have led to the disappearance of traditional middle-class jobs—jobs our education has been making our children ready for.

Since there are more boomerang kids than there are graduates like Gavin, it seems reasonable to say that Gavin is an accident, while the boomerang kids are the norm. In other words, the boomerang kids are the inevitable, while Gavin is a nice serendipity. This is because our traditional education, by design, produces employees rather than entrepreneurs. The challenge for educators today, if we wish to have fewer boomerang kids, is to figure out how to redesign our education to prepare entrepreneurs like Gavin so they do not happen by accident.

THE IDEAL SCHOOL

That is the purpose of the book *World Class Learners: Educating Creative and Entrepreneurial Students*, which outlines a new design that would turn the Gavin accident into institutional arrangement. The design includes three elements:

1. *Personalization:* Changing education from imposing on students the same standardized content to enabling students to pursue their passion and strength through student voice and choice, a broad and flexible curriculum, and mentoring and advising.

2. *Product-oriented learning:* Changing pedagogy from just-in-case knowledge transmitting to just-in-time supporting of students' engagement in entrepreneurial activities aiming to produce authentic products and services.

3. *Globalized campus:* Expanding the educational setting from local, isolated, physical spaces to global and virtual spaces to help students develop global perspectives and global competencies.

These three elements form the basic framework of schooling aimed to cultivate globally competent, creative, and entrepreneurial talents needed today. They are about redesigning the three primary aspects of schooling: curriculum, pedagogy, and context (see Figure 1). The ideal school should provide opportunities and resources to enable students to personalize their educational experiences instead of receiving a uniform standardized, externally prescribed, education diet. That is, rather than imposing on all students the same knowledge and skills and expecting all students master them at the same pace, the school co-constructs a curriculum that follows the students' passions and enhances their strengths. In terms of pedagogy, teachers in the ideal school facilitate student development by supporting and guiding students through an authentic process of creating works that matter to others. To make this possible, the ideal school brings in global resources and engages students in activities that enable students to learn for and with students from all over the world. Simply put, the ideal school is no longer a physical campus.

While the ideal school in the future is to have all three elements implemented, each element can be implemented

Figure 1   Elements of Entrepreneur-Oriented Education

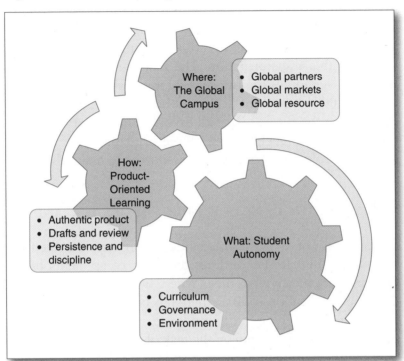

separately. A school or teacher can choose to start working on one of the elements and expand to the other two. The elements can also be implemented at different levels depending on the context. An education system at the district, state, or national level can work at the system level to deliver any or all of the three elements. But a school can do this as well, with the understanding that it can be limited by system level constraints such as a state or national mandated curricula. Even individual teachers can implement the redesigned education in their classrooms, again with the understanding that they are constrained by system and school level factors such as teacher evaluation, mandated curriculum and assessment, as well as availability of resources.

Limited freedom to make changes in a school or classroom is not desirable, but it is better than maintaining the traditional paradigm. The ultimate goal is a complete transformation of schooling from employee-minded education to entrepreneur-minded education. But the realities of education today only allow for a gradual evolutionary approach to realizing this transformation. The fact that we cannot have the ideal version of the future right away should not stop us from acting on pieces of it. We can take baby steps before we leapfrog to the future. Thus all involved in education: policy makers, system level leaders, school principals, and teachers all have a role, the capacity, and resources to make changes.

MAKING THE PARADIGM SHIFT: BOOKS 1, 2, AND 3

World Class Learners presents evidence for why we need the paradigm shift. It also outlines the basic components of the new paradigm as well as areas where we can begin the work. Since its publication in 2012, there has been growing demand for more practice-oriented guidance and support to help schools and teachers take on the task of transforming the outdated education paradigm. In response, we decided to work on three books, each addressing one of the elements of the new paradigm.

Three books are intended to be practical. In other words, *World Class Learners* is about the *why* and *what* of educational paradigm shift; these three books are about the *how* and *what* happens. They are cowritten by researchers and practitioners. They include specific strategies, practical advice, and stories of success and struggle. The strategies, advice, and stories were collected from classrooms and schools that have embarked on the transformation journey. They reflect both promises and challenges of the new paradigm when implemented in the current educational settings. While they are intended to guide and inspire, they are not meant to be prescriptive because each school and classroom has its unique opportunities and constraints.

The organization of the three books is similar. They start with a discussion of theories and definitions of each element, followed by specific suggestions for how each can be implemented and what challenges exist that may work against the implementation. The suggestions are specific to system leaders, school leaders, and classroom teachers. They are also made with the consideration of different realities— thinking (beginning), implementing (intermediate), and expanding (advanced).

Each of the three books addresses one element of the new paradigm. *Personalization and Student Autonomy* provides guidance and suggestions for actions that systems, schools, and classrooms can take to create more autonomy for students and enable them to personalize their educational experiences, to enhance their strengths, and to follow their passions. *Product-Oriented Learning* provides guidance and suggestions for systems, schools, and classrooms to design and develop infrastructures and resources to enable students to engage in authentic projects. *Globalized Campus* is to help schools and teachers develop global engagement activities for students.

1

Product-Oriented Learning

What Is It?

by Yong Zhao

P roduct-oriented learning (POL) is one of the three essential elements of the entrepreneur-oriented education paradigm, together with personalization and global campus. While *personalization* is to transform the *what* of education (i.e., the curriculum dimension), and *global campus* transforms the *where* of education (i.e., the context and setting), *POL* is to transform the *how* of education (i.e., the pedagogy dimension). Product-oriented learning spurs substantive shifts changing learning from just-in-case to just-in-time, teaching from knowledge transmitting to facilitating product making, and learners from consumers to creators.

POL vs. PBL

POL stems from project-based learning or problem-based learning (PBL), but it differs significantly from how PBL has been practiced in most settings. The differences occur in the following five ways: (1) developing the entrepreneurial mindset vs. mastery of content, (2) initiated by student vs. initiated by teacher, (3) strength based vs. deficit driven, (4) quality of final product, and (5) use of final product.

Developing the Entrepreneurial Mindset vs. Mastery of Content

The first significant difference is purpose. PBL is typically about mastery of predetermined academic content and skills. It is used to provide a more engaging learning experience to help students better master the desired learning knowledge and skill as implied by such phrases often associated with PBL as "learning by doing," "learning by making," and "invent to learn." POL is about developing the entrepreneurial mindset, habits, and skills, which can only be developed through authentic entrepreneurial activities. Thus POL is practiced to engage students in producing meaning and valuable works, works that matter to someone. To create a product would certainly result in learning, but what is learned may not fit government-sanctioned standards or curriculum. The PBL phrases would be changed to "learn to do," "learn to make," and "learn to invent" in POL.

In other words, PBL's primary concern is the content and skills prescribed in the curriculum. The project or product is only a vehicle to get to the curricular expectations, thus of secondary concern. Therefore, in most PBL practices, teachers start designing the projects by asking what projects are best suited to teach the desired content and skills. Even when they have an excellent project in mind, they work hard to find a way to demonstrate how it supports acquisition of the prescribed content.

Under POL, the primary concern is the product, the outcome of the project. The extent to which the project may help teach the prescribed content is of secondary or little importance. POL is not constrained by a preset curriculum or standards, so teachers do not have to force a project to fit the curriculum.

Initiated by the Student vs. Initiated by the Teacher

The different purposes lead to the second significant difference between POL and PBL: Who is the initiator? Since PBL's concern is about ensuring all students learn the same prescribed content, teachers typically initiate the projects. They start with what needs to be taught and develop projects deemed most appropriate for teaching the content. They then ask students to participate in the project.

In contrast, POL gives students the opportunity to initiate projects because it is designed to develop entrepreneurial thinking. One of the most important qualities of entrepreneurs is alertness to opportunities or the ability to identify needs. To develop the alertness, POL starts by asking students to identify unmet needs or opportunities to improve existing conditions in a given situation. It then asks students to propose a solution to meet the needs or bring improvement. The proposed solution becomes the driving force for projects to be implemented.

Strength Based vs. Deficit Driven

The third significant difference between POL and PBL is that POL is strength based, while PBL typically is deficit driven. Successful entrepreneurs often capitalize on their strengths and outsource their weakness as a way to differentiate themselves from competitors and maximize the effects of their resources. Thus POL focuses on helping students identify and develop their strengths by asking them how their strengths (passion, ability, social connections, and other resources) contribute to the project. In contrast, PBL aims to ensure that all students learn the same content and meet the same expectations, which often means to fix their deficit—what they are not good at.

Quality of the Final Product

The fourth significant difference is in the process to ensure quality and rigor of the final product. Since PBL is concerned about learning prescribed content, the quality of the final product may not matter at all, provided that the content is covered. POL, on the other hand, aims to develop in students an aspiration to be great instead of just meeting some artificial standards. It also aims to help students understand that greatness comes from sustained and disciplined efforts. Thus POL activities encourage students to be engaged in a process of seeking feedback and continuous revision to improve the quality of their products.

Use of Final Product

Finally, POL differs from PBL in how the final product is used. Very often, PBL products end in a class presentation, school exhibition, or being sent home. But POL products should end with an authentic audience. In other words, POL products have real consumers—people can use the products to improve their lives.

POL: AN ENTREPRENEURIAL EXPERIENCE

POL experiences mimic a typical entrepreneurial activity that includes the following essential steps.

Identify Needs

Alertness to opportunity is an essential element of entrepreneurship. Thus in our attempt to cultivate entrepreneurs, it is essential to help students develop a habit of looking for and the ability to identify opportunities. Opportunities lie in unmet needs and dissatisfaction with the current condition. To develop the habit of discovering opportunities is to cultivate curiosity, unorthodox thinking, and an attitude to challenge the status quo. It is also to cultivate the ability to be empathetic about other people's conditions. Moreover, it is about seeing problems as opportunities and assuming responsibilities for proposing solutions to problems rather than complaining or waiting for someone else to come up with a solution.

To start, the teacher could ask students to make a list of things they are unhappy with in the school, or a condition they are not satisfied with, or an unmet need someone else may have. The teacher could also present a set of unsatisfying conditions, unsolved problems, or unmet needs in different communities. The specific situation can vary, but the over-arching idea is to provide context in which children can find an entrepreneurial opportunity.

Come Up With an Idea

While some students may have an idea right away, many would need to conduct extensive research and work on the need for a while before they can come up with a possible product or service to meet the need. Thus the second essential element is to engage students in the creative and research process that would result in a possible product or service.

Ideas can come from different sources. Students could consult with experts, examine the problem in depth, discuss with peers, or study comparable examples. To stimulate idea creation, the teacher could organize brainstorm sessions, field trips, or expert presentations. The teacher should not assume the entire responsibility for coming up with the idea. In fact, the student should always bear the responsibility for coming up with the idea. The teacher only serves to facilitate the process, create the context, provide resources, and make suggestions.

Assess Strengths and Resources

Once a need is identified and a solution is suggested, entre-preneurs should assess whether they have the capacity and resources to meet the need. This is essentially a process of identifying one's strengths. But the strength does not mean what the student can do at the moment himself or herself. Rather it is what he or she can learn to do and with the help of others. It is also to determine if the need or problem is beyond the capacity and resources available to the student.

Understanding one's weaknesses and strengths is key to entrepreneurial success. We cannot expect all students to have the same abilities. It is thus an important step to provide the opportunity for students to learn how to identify and further enhance their strengths, while avoiding their weaknesses. It is also important to help students understand that they do not have to be equally good at everything, because what is missing in them could be "outsourced" to others, that is, partners. Hence, identifying one's strengths and weaknesses is also to learn about the strengths and weaknesses of others.

Convince Someone

All entrepreneurs need to convince others of the value of their products or services, be it an investor, a partner, or someone who may work for them. Thus the product-oriented learning experience should include the requirement for students to convince others that the needs they identified are significant, the products they proposed are of value and feasible, and someone will "buy" what they produce. To do so, they may need to develop a business plan and make a public presentation in or outside the school to "sell" their ideas.

The stage of convincing someone may go beyond one single session because if the students fail to convince, they will need to revise their ideas and plans. The idea of multiple drafts, critique, and peer review is applicable at this stage as well as at the stage of product making.

Make the Product or Service

Once the proposed idea is accepted, students move on to the product-making stage, which is similar to the project enactment stage in traditional project-based learning. At this stage, students work on their products as proposed, individually or in teams. To help improve the quality of the final product, the same process of "multiple drafts and critique" should be used. It is also desirable to seek the involvement of professionals as reviewers and mentors and to apply professional standards to all products and services.

Market the Product

Once the product is made, the students need to market it to its intended audience. Learning to market their products can help students better understand what is required to be an entrepreneur as well as the real needs of the world. The results may be a huge success or a complete failure. Either way, the experience can help students develop essential entrepreneurial competences—reflection, resilience, confidence, communication, and perseverance.

Marketing is also the stage when students learn marketing skills and marketing tools. Depending on the specific product and intended customers, students need to engage in marketing activities using a variety of media and venues. They could use social media such as Twitter and Facebook, traditional media such as posters, or talk to the customers face-to-face.

Post-Product Management and Maintenance

The product-oriented learning cycle does not end with marketing. In some cases, students have to manage the sales and maintenance of the product. They may also need to upgrade the products, for example, in cases of software (e.g., a computer game). Or they may have to manage an online store that sells their products and maintain communication with users.

POL: SUMMARY

To summarize, because it aims to cultivate entrepreneurial spirit and skills, the POL places more emphasis on the end products or services. They must not only be of high quality but also have appeal to an external audience. In POL, the students are in more control of the project. They propose and initiate the project. They need to convince the teacher to approve the project and, if needed, convince their peers to become partners.

And for that, they need to create a business plan, complete with documentations and analyses of targeted audience and needs, a feasibility analysis, and marketing strategies. The teacher, in this model, serves as the "venture capitalist," who helps decide if the project is needed and feasible; the consultant, who provides suggestions and resources on demand; the motivator, who encourages at times of disappointment; the focus group, which provides feedback and critique on prototypes; and the partner, who provides complementary expertise and skills. The teacher or other adults could bring opportunities, help identify needs, make connections to potential customers, or make suggestions for potential projects because of the expertise and social capital—but ultimately, it is the students who should decide what products to make. In the mixed model, projects are often group based, that is, a group (an entire class, for example) of students works on the same project. In the entrepreneurial model, projects can be group based, but they can also be individually initiated.

The setting for POL can be individual classes, but more often than not, it requires a platform and culture at the school level for a number of reasons. First, in order to create high-quality products, students will most likely need large chunks of time beyond what a typical class period can offer. Second, the students will also need to have access to expertise beyond what one individual teacher could have. In some cases, such expertise may reside outside the school. Third, the knowledge and skills required to create authentic products would not fit nicely with one single school subject. Fourth, students will need some platform or venue to have access to potential customers. Finally, some students may be engaged in a project or service that is exceptionally time consuming, which would necessitate making special arrangement in terms of school scheduling.

POL: CHALLENGES

POL shows a significant departure from traditional teaching, even from the new model of traditional teaching: PBL. It undoubtedly presents tremendous challenges to teachers and schools. This book brings examples to illustrate strategies and recommendations to help schools and teachers interested in adopting POL to cultivate entrepreneurial students.

QUESTIONS FOR YOU TO CONSIDER

Here are a few questions adapted from a World Class School Report Card (Zhao, 2012) for you to consider as you create a climate and culture of POL in your classroom and school.

- Is there an infrastructure in your school for students to develop, display, or market products and services?
- Are relevant policies that govern student products in place? For example, policies regarding ownership of intellectual property, patents, etc.?
- What products and services have students created?
- In what ways have the products and services of students been used?
- To what degree are students engaged in product-oriented learning?
- What percentage of student enrichment activities is product oriented?
- Is there an established process for reviewing proposals and products?
- Is there an established process and protocol for product improvement?
- Is there an established process to engage external experts from the broad community to participate in proposal and product review?
- Are there established criteria for products and proposal review?

REFERENCES

Zhao, Y. (2012). *World class learners: Educating creative and entrepreneurial students* (1st ed.). Thousand Oaks, CA: Corwin.

2

Projects With a Purpose

Finding an Authentic Audience

by Emily McCarren

"I believe that education is a process of living, not preparation for future living."

—John Dewey

"[A]s a platform for marketing, technology makes it possible for students to reach a global audience for their products."

—Zhao (2012, p. 254)

"This is one salient characteristic of an 'authentic assessment': it is designed to provide the student with a genuine rather than a contrived learning experience that provides both the teacher and student with opportunities to learn what the student can do. The demonstration of learning occurs in a situation that requires the application and production of knowledge rather than the mere recognition or reproduction of correct answers."

—Darling-Hammond (1995, pp. 3–4)

Featured School

Student Global Leadership
Institute at Punahou School, Honolulu, HI

A group of 80 high school students from all over the world are gathered for a large conference, discussing health issues in their communities. The students spent the first several days of the 2-week institute getting to know each other, listening to global health experts, and trying to uncover the issues in their communities that could be served by their passions, interest, and expertise. Chai Reddy, the lead teacher for the Student Global Leadership Institute at Punahou School in Honolulu, Hawaii, challenged the students: "You are not here for yourself, you are here to gain global insight into the topic of health and return to your communities to improve the lives of at least one person there."

Anna, Filippa, and Hanna, from Viktor Rydberg Gymnasium Odenplan, a high school in Stockholm, Sweden, listened carefully to their peers from the United States, Japan, the United Kingdom, China, Singapore, and Jordan, not just during the formal elements of the program, but on the margins of the conference as well. On the bus, touring the island, late at night in the dorms, the girls began to notice a disturbing reality related to the topic of health, something common to each of these students from diverse global communities: stress in schools. Throughout the 2 weeks of the Institute, they discussed their ideas with their colleagues, tried to understand the topic from diverse viewpoints, and engaged with mentors from the local business community who guided them in project scope and planning and management, and experts in the field of health sciences.

At the end of the 2 weeks, the three girls presented a proposal to explore and make an impact on stress in their school and community. When they returned to Sweden, they spent a good deal of the fall conducting interviews with students and experts in the community, all chronicled in a blog, "Bringing a Little Aloha Back to VRG" (Enström, Martinsson, & Bielawska Bokliden, 2013). In September 2012, the team wrote this on their blog: "We would like for something productive to come out of our research. Something you can lay your hands on. Something that brings more attention to the actual subject. Some sort of product." At that moment in the process, they felt they were really on to something.

Their idea was to create a magnetic game board that could be posted on the fridge at home, and family members would move their magnets around the board to demonstrate how they were dealing with stress. Did you go to bed on time? Move forward two spaces. Did you attend a hosted meditation session at school? Move forward three spaces. Have self-deprecating thoughts about your academic ability? Move back two.

For various reasons, the students decided not to pursue the product concept and continued the complex—and more traditionally academic—work of analyzing and coding the qualitative data they collected through their surveys and interviews. They were not surprised to discover that some of their hunches were right: School and the associated pressure (or perceived pressure) to perform at a high level was a significant cause of student stress. In addition to their work in Sweden, they connected with another group that attended the Institute at Punahou—a boys' school in Japan—that was following a similar inquiry about school-related stress and also wondering what action would impact the issue. Together, the two teams collected additional data from all of the students who had participated in the Institute, generating a dataset that would be the envy of a university graduate student.

Based on their research, the girls in Sweden proposed a number of interventions for the school to consider, such as school-facilitated group study sessions, increased access to a school counselor, and meditation programs. And they even piloted a few to get feedback from the community. At the end of the year, and the conclusion of their project, they wrote a thoughtful report of their findings and reflected on what they thought the next steps should be.

By all accounts, they had met and even exceeded the expectations of the Institute. But in the paradigm of product-oriented learning, this was a missed opportunity. They produced a report that was read by their teacher, but they missed the chance to produce something that had a deep impact on the people they sought to help. These girls did everything that was asked of them and more: They researched, and they engaged in deep empathy with the community they were seeking to help and understand. But despite all these efforts, no social change came out of their work. Their own knowledge of the topic was deepened, which is not to be dismissed, but they were not pushed to make an authentic impact through their learning. They reported the reality to a single person, and then they were done.

Principles for Finding
an Authentic Audience

- Redefine your audience
- Define your purpose
- Articulate your process
- Identify your audience
- Make a difference locally
- Identify needs
- Come up with a solution: Identify the product and purpose

Redefine Your Audience

An essential element in understanding product-oriented learning is to think about audience and purpose. In schools, there is a huge amount of tangible evidence of student work and learning: recycling bins, boxes, computer drives overflow with this evidence. There is also the more ephemeral evidence: the conversations, the looks of astonishment, the moments that teachers might have the joy of observing, but fail to capture on video or audio. In kindergarten, the evidence might be a book made by a student at a writing center, a block structure built, or a conflict between classmates peacefully resolved. In middle or high school, we might see students' notes, their tests, or projects they have completed.

In a highly personalized learning environment, like the one created in the Student Global Leadership Institute, there will be lots going on and plenty of evidence of learning; this was certainly true in Filippa, Hanna, and Anna's case. Their blog and the reports that they produced are evidence of the thinking they did and the good process they pursued. There is no shortage of products created in schools. However, what this approach calls for are products that have a purpose beyond student learning, and an audience beyond the teacher. Work that is created for the teacher alone is wasted work. Yet in the traditional paradigm of schooling, the concept of busy work, which has no real purpose or lasting value and does not support learning, is an everyday reality. It would be interesting if it became commonplace for teachers to ask students in their classes: "Have you thought about what it would take to develop your ideas into a sustainable business effort?" Or, "I like what you wrote in your reading journal last week. How might I help you build a nonprofit around the ideals you are exploring?"

In personalized learning, we leave the inquiry, the process, and even the product up to the students. But that does not mean that they are completely on their own: Teachers and schools should be unrelenting in insisting that the work of their students serve the community (however you choose to define that) and be of high quality. Teachers have the important responsibility to expose students to contexts in which they can contribute and make a difference. How student learning ultimately serves others will manifest in many different ways, and the insistence that it will serve others must be present in all learning environments. A core value of the World Class Learners paradigm is that students will develop the habit of looking around the world and asking: How can I help?

> Opportunities lie in unmet needs and dissatisfaction with the current condition . . . . [I]t is about seeing problems as opportunities and assuming responsibility for proposing solutions to problems rather than complaining or waiting for someone else to come up with a solution. (Zhao, 2012, p. 205)

How do we expose our students to communities and environments rich with interesting problems to solve? Teachers and students don't have to look far to find places where people have needs that they can address in a positive way—they can start (like Filippa, Anna, and Hana did) with their school. Schools of all types, all over the world, are hotbeds of opportunity for product oriented learning.

Define Your Purpose

Filippa, Hanna, and Anna were doing sophisticated research about an important topic and had been challenged to make a difference in their community, and they did good work. Imagine the impact they might have had if they had been more explicit in determining an audience and purpose for their work. Throughout the year, their blog posts express that they are doing this work, and reflecting on it for the mentors and teachers who are supporting them. There are several posts about word count compliance in the report that might make a progressive educator cringe. This example has incredibly talented students working on a hugely important topic, but their work is missing audience and purpose. They did not produce a product for the community; they produced a product (an excellent one, in the traditional academic paradigm) for their teacher. Their product served their learning, but imagine if, in addition, it had a significant impact on their fellow students. They missed out on that powerful outcome because the concept of audience was not clear to them as a necessary outcome of their work. The absence of this expectation is absolutely the norm in most schooling environments.

Articulate Your Process

At any grade level, the genesis of product-based learning goes back to empathy and ethics. Producing products, for your company, or to demonstrate and expand learning, always starts with understanding what people want, feel, and need—this is empathy. The first thing that a teacher or leader needs to do is figure out how to expose students to the needs of others. Again, this can begin in your own classroom or school, or reach as far as a community on the other side of the planet. The process in the Student Global Leadership Institute is simple: Students spend 2 weeks immersed in the global reality of a particular pressing theme. They are learning about their own strengths as community leaders and also about a topic that desperately needs the attention of the most eager and ambitious leaders of the next generation. The students in the Institute are then challenged to figure out what action they will take, what product they will produce, and for whom. They need to find the audience, the question, or a pressing need and a solution or change that they can bring about. On the final day of the Institute, student teams present their plans to their peers and determine how to complete their work, supported by coordinating teachers from their home schools. In any learning environment at any age, students should be identifying their strengths and passions and constantly considering how those same strengths and passions can serve the needs of others. The field of marketing is a good place to look if your students (or you as the teacher) need help finding audiences. The Web is full of marketing primers, blogs, and instructional videos designed to help entrepreneurs find their audience. At the time of print, Coursera offers an introduction to marketing MOOC (massive open online course) in collaboration with the Wharton School of Business at the University of Pennsylvania (Coursera Marketing Course, n.d.). Teachers or high school students, or even particularly precocious middle school students, could take the course together and form a team of expert consultants at your school to help other students find their audiences.

Make a Difference Locally

Before going that far, you might ask: What can students create, build, make, or design that would improve something at your school? Maybe people are dissatisfied with school lunches, or the sound of the bells, or the traffic on the way to school in the morning, or the clumsy design of the furniture in the English classrooms. Schools are ripe with opportunity for change, in small and large ways. Whatever the problem is, consider the first step: defining the audience. Who is the audience? Who are we designing for? Proponents of design-thinking methodology will recognize this as an essential element of the design process. Design thinking encourages designers to identify outliers or strange cases to better understand and then design for, suggesting that if you design for normal you will rarely innovate. Whatever process you use, you cannot skip the step of identifying your audience. And remember this essential caveat: We are trying to broaden the audience of student work. So whenever possible and reasonable, the audience should not just be the evaluating teacher.

Filippa, Anna, and Hanna, the brilliant students from Sweden, knew who their audience was and who they wanted to design solutions for: their overworked peers whose health was suffering because of the stress of school and its associated pressures. Throughout the project, they continually reflected on their desire to make a change for current and future students in their own school, and also their new friends all over the world. And then, at the critical moment of their yearlong, thorough, and careful work (at the risk of hyperbole), they turned their backs on their peers and turned in a paper to their teacher. Imagine the impact if they had kept a sharp focus on improving the experience of just one person, just one stressed out student. Instead, they retreated to the academic norm and designed a final product (the research paper) for their teachers.

In schools, teachers can encourage students to seek broader audiences for their work, not only via traditional venues such as science fairs or debates, but also as meaningful and targeted agents of change. And remember, at many points in the learning process, students themselves are, in fact, their own meaningful audience: They can be challenged to create something that is deeply pleasing to them, and of which they are very proud. While one's self can be an authentic audience in any and all subject areas, it often emerges in the performing arts when students, individually and in groups, find deep joy and gratitude in their music, dance, or theatre productions. The concept of authentic and meaningful audience does not seek to undermine the essential role of doing things because you love them and they make you feel like a more complete person.

Table 2.1   Some Possible Audiences for Student Work

The Student Himself or Herself	In the School Community	In the Local Government
	Fellow students Other classes or student organizations Head of school School board Cafeteria or grounds staff Parents	Department of sanitation Parks Department Department of Land and Natural Resources Elected officials
In Community Agencies and Organizations Homeless shelters Community centers Retirement communities Preschools Other nonprofit organizations	**Online Audiences (national and global reach)** Online discussion forums Online conferences Twitter chats Global collaborations	**Businesses** Local businesses National businesses Pitch to a Venture Capital Firm Seek to raise funds for manufacturing on Kickstarter or other crowdsourcing websites Engage with local start-up incubators to test and get feedback on student-led ideas

Table 2.2   Some Things Students Can Create for Their Audiences

Services	Media	Things
Tutoring Peer counseling	Print or electronic materials Op-ed pieces in the paper Presence in social media Websites Instructional videos Online courses or modules Consortiums for language exchange Games	Inventions Art

Identify Needs

Depending on a number of factors—student age, desired learning outcomes, and others—the teacher may find that students come up with solutions to problems prior to defining the audience. This is not an insurmountable issue. While one role of the teacher is to ensure that the students are not imposing things on communities that don't need them, it is an appropriate learning challenge to ask students, "Okay, you came up with this, where is it needed, and by whom?"

Teachers in middle and high school might use the spoof fundraising campaign video called "Africa for Norway." In the short video, the well-meaning Africans send radiators to Norway to save the Norwegians from the frigid climate. In the video, the Africans sing that "we have heat enough for Norway, it's time for us to share" (Radi-aid, 2012). This comedic parody criticizes the status quo on a number of levels. First, the extent to which things (shoes, school supplies, and clothes) get sent to communities in nations all over Africa without any sense of what the particular community actually needs. And second, the idea that because one community has something does not mean every community in the world wants it. Starting with the audience and its needs, then, is not only more efficient and more likely to have an impact, but also more ethical.

For example, you may have a student who is passionate about improving the lives of elderly people. For them, the audience is the first step, and then they have to move on to identifying the need: How can that student's strengths and passions make an impact on the life of a particular elderly person or community? Other students might start with an issue, such as the need for increased understanding about energy conservation in their community. Then they have to find an audience for whom they can design their product. With a little practice, helping students identify needs will become second nature to teachers.

In more open-ended inquiry, students could study the methods of business and advertising focus groups and explore themes through interviews with representatives of their desired audience. Or they might use social media to engage in empathy, turning to Twitter, Facebook or other platforms where their audience is already engaged to take polls or connect with people in far-flung communities about the topic they are exploring. There are few topics about which you can't get nearly instant feedback via social media, so teachers should leverage these technologies to engage in real time with the people their students' work is intended to serve.

Come Up With a Solution: Identify the Product and Purpose

Once the audience and need are determined, the students, through empathy, need to come up with entrepreneurial solutions to the issues their audience is facing. In this realm, the Swedish team really thrived. They were excellent empathetic learners, listening carefully to their audience (fellow students) in their well-designed research process. In the process of discovering solutions, students need to be challenged to be creative and, again, to look at their strengths. What talents, skills, and interests can they use to improve the situation they have identified? What service can they provide, or what product can they make, that will answer the need for the identified audience?

The senior Capstone Course (n.d.) at the Punahou School in Honolulu, Hawaii, is a social studies course that grew out of economics and community service course requirements. Students spend time, over the course of a semester, volunteering in a community organization and learning about the needs of the population served by that organization. They also spend time reflecting on their capacities to have an impact in that or a related area in the community. The students are challenged to take action based on their own strengths and community needs. The projects vary from the compliant to the inspired. One of the biggest challenges for students in this course is that the final product is not predetermined. They are seniors in their last year of secondary school throughout which, most of the time, they have been told exactly what the outcomes should look like. When they are finally asked to look inward at their own strengths and passions and then out beyond the school gates to the community, they can find themselves feeling untethered and in unfamiliar territory.

Many fine schools have analogous courses or programs, or community engagement incentives or requirements. The question that this book is asking is how do we move this to the core, and not have it be an afterthought to our general curriculum, or a Capstone experience that our curriculum has not prepared them for. How might helping people (in the school, locally, and globally) in new, creative, innovative, and entrepreneurial ways be the foundation for our work in schools, not just the window dressing? Surely, finding those people that our students' work will serve is an important challenge in this work. What follows are some more strategies for identifying this crucial audience of student work at the class, school, and district levels.

More Strategies for Focusing on Audience and Purpose

In the Classroom

As classroom teachers, even if no one else in your school has heard of product-oriented learning, you can have a significant impact by considering the audiences for your students' work.

Reframe the Historical Context (Beginning-Intermediate)

To start, take a unit that you teach in your class and reframe it through the "audience and need" paradigm. For example, in a traditional class on U.S. history in a high school, we will often see a one-size-fits-all approach: Essay tests and traditional essay assignments are the norm. If a personalized approach is being taken, perhaps the students are determining what they wish to learn about the American Revolution, for example, and are given choice and opportunity about how to demonstrate their learning. But to whom are they going to demonstrate that learning? If they have been engaged in determining an area of exploration and then completed some sort of assessment of their learning, the fruit of their labor might be a few comments in the margins from the teacher. The teacher, mind you, is not learning or gaining from the consumption of that product (be it an essay, a video, a poster, an interpretative dance). At best, they might be entertained, which is not to be minimized in its importance, but it is not something the teacher really needs or benefits from in any meaningful way. In fact, he or she may have even seen similar products before. (He or she may even be so savvy as to be employing technology such as turnitin. com to ensure that an essay product is the students' work and not that of another author.) But what is the purpose of the students' work? Why did they spend the time, and for whom?

If we reframe audience, things can change quite quickly. The students in the U.S. history class are developing knowledge in the field, they are reading, reflecting, exploring, and making meaning. How might this work be of service in the world? While it might seem utopian at first, with a little bit of creative thinking the possibilities start to unfold. Imagine a class on U.S. history at a university in England (or high school, although it is not a widely taught subject in secondary schools).

What if the students in the class were invited to create products (a website, blog posts, historical figure Twitter feeds, an instructional video) aimed at teaching their peers in England about the subject? You can imagine how the engagement would increase instantly; when students are presenting to an audience larger than just the teacher, quality, excitement, and motivation are all increased. Not to mention intellectual rigor: To understand how to tell the story, you would have to know that it might be known as the American War of Independence, and you would bring higher stakes to a review process knowing that you were not just checking off a box on a rubric that requires review, but actually taking an opportunity to make the work more presentable to your international audience.

Reframe How You Describe
the Work of Your Class (Implementing)

Set up your syllabus by themes and allow students to determine what they want to learn in each theme and set them loose to identify needs and audiences to create for, based on the themes. You might run a process similar to the popular reality TV show *Shark Tank* and invite entrepreneurs from the community to come to your class (in person or via videoconference) to critique the products that your students have created. In your class, tell your students that they will be evaluated (by you, their peers and all the people they will be "working" for) based on the impact that their work has. Let them know that there is no easy A in your class—that to be excellent they have to have an impact, not just jump through hoops. With your students, create a system that earns points for the widest reach of your schoolwork. Perhaps in a Spanish class, to earn an outstanding grade, a student's audience has to serve people in a Spanish speaking community.

Implement Guerrilla Cross-Disciplinary Teams (Expanding)

If you are a radical, product-oriented learning guru, and you still cannot convince the powers-that-be to create the flexible schedule and interdisciplinary opportunities for your students, do it yourself! Establish a cohort of teachers at your school dedicated to this concept and look for ways that you can collaborate to shift expectations of the traditional paradigm (tests, homework, and class time) for students that you have in common. Encourage your students to take on a big project and agree that they can get credit in English *and* Physics. Be liberal in your sense of fairness, understanding that different processes, outcomes, and even expectations for different students are not just permissible, but an essential piece of cultivating World Class Learners.

In the School and School System

(Leaders) Provide Teacher Training (Thinking)

Product-oriented learning is another way to think about assessment of student learning. At the district level and school level, leaders should provide training for teachers interested in exploring this paradigm and also clearly communicate that it is something valued and allowed. One of the greatest barriers to the deeply valuable and authentic learning opportunities that will result from this method is teachers' fear that they are not allowed to do it. Invite experimentation and celebrate teachers who are pushing themselves and their students in this work.

To move forward the notion of authentic audiences, host roundtable discussions for teachers and encourage groups of educators to share how they have expanded their view of audience for their students' learning.

Share Districtwide Resources,
Procedures, and Norms (Beginning-Implementing)

Generate lists of organizations in the community that are eager to work with students and provide them to teachers. Similarly, when needed, adjust your social media policies such that they encourage your teachers to engage on social media and support their students (where age appropriate) to leverage social media to find and engage with authentic audiences for their work and learning.

Create Venues for Sharing Meaningful
Student Work at the District Level (Beginning)

Find some excellent examples of product-oriented learning in your district and find ways to honor that publicly. Present it to the school board, blog about it, present at professional conferences, and share widely that this is the hallmark of the excellent learning environment at your schools. This will proliferate the sense of permission that educators so desperately need, and as this kind of learning becomes the norm, more and more community organizations will reveal themselves as potential audiences for your students' work.

Redefine the Schedule (Implementing)

As schools begin to learn the language of product-oriented learning, system leadership can begin to shift structures that will more easily facilitate this kind of learning, creating space in schedules for interdisciplinary learning opportunities by giving students credit in multiple departments for products that they successfully create. Also, redefining the schedule will give students increased access to the audiences for whom their products are intended. For example, a particular class (or, even better, group of classes) could shift some of its "class time" online so that students could learn asynchronously, working at their own pace, and the time together in class becomes all about finding audiences and learning from them, engaging with guest speakers from all over the community (local or global) to move projects and ideas forward.

Redefine the Core Expectations (Expanding)

At the highest level of transformation, schools might specialize around pressing issues and needs. Perhaps instead of Grades 9–12, there are labs in the school that students can join that are looking at different issues globally. Students can move through the labs or stay in one for 4 years. There might be one lab looking at global health, one looking at resource management or environmental sustainability, and another looking at diplomacy and international relations. The work of identifying needs and audiences could be framed within the greater themes, allowing students to learn based on their passions and strengths while having their learning be in service to others. In this model, you can imagine student-initiated business and products becoming the norm with each graduating class.

OVERCOMING CHALLENGES

The challenge to look to authentic audiences for our student work can seem daunting—lack of time required to cultivate the relationships required, lack of support throughout the school, lack of models in a school or district, and so on. But the costs of not doing this are high. Creating the opportunity for students to feel that their work matters, that they are heard, that their voice matters in the world, not just in a classroom, is one of the most meaningful gifts that an educator can give their students. And one of the most rewarding opportunities for educators is to fully realize the value that their students can add to the world, not some day in the distant future when they are "done" with school, but now, as part of the important work of learning that they do every day. Take a few moments to consider the reasons that leveraging authentic audiences is important for your students and their experience in school, and then imagine what role, small or large, you will play in supporting their authentic learning.

ACTIVITY #1: IDENTIFYING AND NAMING OUR FEARS WITH AUTHENTIC AUDIENCES

Participants: Teachers and administrators

Objective: This activity allows teachers to suspend their hesitations and perceived barriers to engaging authentic audiences for their student work and also provides a space for honoring their hesitations and sense of what is good for children.

Materials

- Butcher paper
- Poster board (a whiteboard is fine too, but if you use paper and these discussions are ongoing, you can bring the "Parking Lot" to subsequent meetings for re-use)
- Markers

Process: After reading the chapter, have teachers gather in small groups and name the barriers for finding authentic audiences for student work. Post them on butcher paper or poster board on a corner of the room. Label the poster "Parking Lot."

This is not saying that these fears are not valid but that we will not focus on them in the generative discussions to come.

Reflection: As a group or individually, consider the barriers that have been shared.

- Are there different types of barriers? Perhaps some are emotional, some are based on fear of failure or expo-sure, some are about existing norms or structures in the school schedule.
- Are there barriers that are based on a fixed mindset about what school should look like? See if as individu-als or a group you can divide them into categories to better understand them.
- Finally, and most importantly, consider the process for removing some of these barriers—who has to engage in making this happen? Are there ways that permission can be given for the barriers to be removed?

ACTIVITY #2: THE VALUE OF AN AUTHENTIC AUDIENCE

Participants: Teachers

Objective: To give teachers a window into how authentic audience can improve engagement and the quality of student work.

Materials

- Blank 8 x 11 paper
- Markers, other paper craft supplies

Process

(2 minutes) Welcome teachers and pass out two pieces of blank paper to each teacher. Have colorful markers and craft supplies available, but not at each table.

(5 minutes) Instruct the teachers, on the first piece of paper, to draw a picture that represents their educational philosophy (see alternate prompts below). Let them know this will be just for their own use and they can crumple it up at the end of the 5 minutes of drawing time. Let them know that supplies are available at the side table. Have them fold it up or flip it over, but do not dispose of it.

(5 minutes) Now, let the teachers know that on their next piece of paper, they will do the same activity, but these will be posted in the entrance to school tomorrow (or some high visibility place for students and their colleagues to see). Remind them that supplies are available at the side table.

[Alternate question: What do you care most about in your work as a teacher? Draw a picture that represents the class that you teach. Create an image that expresses what you hope for your students' futures.]

Reflection: (5–30 minutes or online discussion)

> How did you feel while you were completing the first task?
>
> How did you feel completing the second task?
>
> If there was a difference, why do you think that was?
>
> When your students are asked to complete work, who is their audience?

ACTIVITY #3: FINDING ONLINE CONNECTIONS

Participants: Teachers and administrators

(30 minutes–1 hour)

Objective: To help teachers see the wealth of resources available to them as audiences for their students.

Materials/Setting

- Devices with Internet connection
- Given the learning outcomes of your class, what are some organizations that could make good use of student-generated content? These might be schools, NGOs, non-profits (museums, retirement communities, community centers), or government run entities (community centers, preschool programs, local utilities, or waste management companies)

Process

1. In groups of two to three, find as many possibilities as you can in 15 minutes. Don't focus on probable links; think wildly and expansively.

    What might be some unexpected possibilities?

    What might be some possibilities most likely to get your class on the local news?

    What might be some possibilities that would gain notice from national or international media?

2. Give each group 1–2 minutes to share out some things that they found.

Reflection: If the expectation was that students were creating products or content for others, what would have to change in our school system? In our classes? What are small steps that we can take as teachers, tomorrow, to move toward this goal?

REFERENCES

Capstone Program at Punahou School. (n.d.). Retrieved from http://www.punahou.edu/bulletin/detail/index.aspx?linkid=794&moduleid=69

Coursera Marketing Course. (n.d.). https://www.coursera.org/course/whartonmarketing

Darling-Hammond, L. (1995). *Authentic assessment in action: Studies of schools and students at work.* New York, NY: Teachers College Press.

Enström, A., Martinsson, F., & Bielawska Bokliden, H. (2013). *Bringing a Little Aloha Back to VRG.* Retrieved from alohavrg .weebly.com

Radi-aid. (2012). Africa for Norway. Retrieved from http://www .africafornorway.no/

Zhao, Y. (2012). *World class learners: Educating creative and entrepreneurial students* (1st ed.). Thousand Oaks, CA: Corwin.

3

Quality Products That Speak for Themselves

Processes for Review and Revision, Student Evaluation, and Assessment

by Kay Tucker

"*Because it aims to cultivate the entrepreneurial spirit and skills, the entrepreneurial model places more emphasis on the artifacts: the end products or services. They must not only be of high quality but also have appeal to an external audience: customers. The product or service must meet an authentic need of the customer, who is willing to put in resources (time, energy, or money) for the product or service.*"

—Zhao (2012, pp. 202–203)

Featured Student

Chloe Maxmin
Lincoln Academy, Newcastle, ME

Chloe Maxmin has a personal mission that is powerful—to make climate change the defining issue of her generation. This mission started at a young age and has evolved and grown over the years.

> When I was twelve, I learned that the largest real estate devel-
> oper in the country—Plum Creek—wanted to build marinas, golf
> courses, hundreds of house lots, and helipads all over Maine's
> pristine North Woods. I knew that the proposal could not go
> through, so I took action. (Maxmin, 2015)

She joined local environmental groups, testified at public hearings, and wrote articles for the local papers. Chloe's mission followed her to high school—Lincoln Academy, Maine—where as a freshman she formed a club to inspire her classmates to join her in efforts to stop the Plum Creek development. She also realized that there was little awareness of environmental issues among her peers and limited action being taken by the school and community to prevent global warming. To counter this, she founded the Climate Action Club (CAC) and helped script many environmental initiatives using multiple approaches to reduce the carbon footprint of the school and the community. These actions won the club an award from Youth Venture and Earth Island Institute enabling Chloe and several other students to attend an environmental boot camp at the University of Florida—a 3-day workshop on sustainability. This drew attention from the Sundance Channel's environmental programming, and they included Chloe in a segment of "Big Ideas for a Small Planet—Communities" (n.d.).

This was only the beginning of her pathway leading to the creation of a website (service) that empowers and helps students make a difference in their communities by countering climate change. First Here, Then Everywhere (FHTE) is a forum for young people to connect, get help, support, and advice with their ventures. Every month, she showcases a new youth-led venture working to mitigate climate change. As stated on the website, the mission of First Here, Then Everywhere "will

(Continued)

(Continued)

spread across the country and the world, motivating teenagers to stand up and act. Collectively, our actions will affect long-lasting positive change" (First Here, Then Everywhere, n.d.).

Perform a search on Chloe Maxmin to find that her journey eventually took her to Harvard where she was action driven every step of the way. She scripted a path of experiences and actions that have allowed her to be involved in multiple ventures, and she has been deemed one of the most influential young "green" activists and environmental leaders of her time. As her experiences and knowledge grew, as the earth changed, and as communities changed, Chloe's approach to healing the planet changed as well. Her mission remains the same, yet her success lies in the fact that she does not take on a one-and-done approach. She reviews current needs and revises what she is doing to take advantage of the issues and trends that will allow her to continue to lead her generation. After all, she firmly believes, "The responsibility to mitigate climate change, change human behavior, and heal the planet will fall to us" (Maxmin, 2015).

PRINCIPLES FOR CREATING A QUALITY PRODUCT

When considering how to continually grow ideas and impact a global audience, it becomes obvious that to develop and maintain a viable product or service, constant revisions must take place. Analyzing and assessing is a major aspect of success. Following are several key principles that apply when creating a quality product and when assessing the developed skills and content that have been uncovered by the student in the process:

- Review and revise to ensure quality and enable a vision to come alive.
- Employ real-world tools for goal setting and product analysis.
- Involve students in assessing the process as well as the product.
- Involve real-world experts in the review and assessment process.

Review and Revise to Ensure
Quality and Enable a Vision to Come Alive

(See Activity #3: Create Strategies for Successful Review and Revision Processes)

When passions drive what students do, as in the case of Chloe Maxmin, the passion itself can be the impetus to continually review and revise the product or service to meet the needs of customers, as well as the vision of the innovator. As Yong Zhao believes, quality products should reflect evidence of multiple drafts, critiques, peer reviews and revisions, as well as feedback from real-world experts. This recurring process ensures that our students come up with and test many ideas instead of settling on the first one—it ensures they fine-tune their efforts based on feedback. The effective learning that takes place in the making process results from a hands-on approach to problem solving, with the added value of the expertise of others.

In schools, however, this important process of the actual making of a product or service is also the area in which teachers and students struggle the most—it is a commitment to large chunks of time and seemingly repetitive efforts. This is the stage where students may fail and want to give up, but also where the learning happens if they are effectively coached to try new things and to persevere. The importance of this process can be seen at NoTosh where one of the steps in their design thinking framework for schools includes ideation, prototyping, and feedback. "The emphasis is on thinking skills and mindsets that allow students to create early and often, adjusting the course of their learning with feedback from peers and the teacher" (NoTosh, n.d.).

We want our students to come up with and test many ideas instead of settling on the first idea they come up with. We want them to learn deeply and be able to apply their thinking to new ideas. We want them to be able to proactively adjust their thinking and their learning pathway to better align with a goal. The process is cyclical but worth establishing as a standard of practice in classrooms and schools. There is not a set way to run through this process, and there are no standard amounts of times to cycle through the process—the key is in allowing the time and in having the tools and strategies in place to empower students and facilitate them through the process in a personalized manner.

Employ Real-World Tools for Goal Setting and Product Analysis

As the aim in this model is to cultivate the entrepreneurial spirit and skills of students, using tools that are used in the workforce is a viable action.

Help Students Create SMART Goals

(See Activity #1: Get SMART!)

> *"Many people fail in life, not for lack of ability or brains or even courage, but simply because they have never organised their energies around a goal."*
>
> —Elbert Hubbard, American philanthropist

> *"SMART is a mnemonic acronym, giving criteria to guide in the setting of objectives, for example in project management, employee-performance management and personal development. The letters S and M usually mean specific and measurable."*
>
> —SMART Criteria (2015)

In an Edutopia post, Maurice Elias, professor of psychology and director of Rutgers Social-Emotional Learning Lab, talks about the importance of students setting SMART goals: "[I]t is an excellent idea to begin school by having our students set positive goals. More and more K–16 schools are introducing concepts like SMART goals as a way of gradually building students' capacity to tackle the increasing challenges they are facing" (Elias, 2014).

In particular, setting SMART goals is very relevant in product-oriented learning. It can be the tool that helps keep students on course with action, measurable results and timelines. Since this strategy is used both to drive success in businesses and to achieve personal goals, it is especially applicable when guiding and assessing students. Take for instance a young lady whose vision is to create a viable blog for kids using technology. The name and logo have been created, shortened urls and QR codes point others to the blog, and there are several posts with visuals and videos. However, the product has few customers, and it could be better and serve a needed purpose with more content and increased exposure and interaction. Having this student create and work on a SMART goal could be the starting point to refocus and reignite inspiration for the project. A possible SMART goal could be:

> Over the next two weeks, I will increase the content and visibility of my tech blog by writing three new posts. I will create and connect both a Twitter and Instagram account to my blog site and broadcast interesting attention grabbers as reasons to visit my site and read my blogs.

Having students think about and take ownership for specific actions leading to a goal will not only provide them with a valuable skill, but will be an important step in the revision and review process leading to the final creation and/ or implementation of products and services. This same goal setting will be a constructive part of the product maintenance aspect of product-oriented learning as well.

Teach Students to Use a SWOT Analysis

(See Activity #2: SWOT it out!)

When organizations consider whether or not a venture will be feasible, they evaluate the product or service using strategies such as the SWOT analysis (Strengths, Weaknesses, Opportunities, and Threats). They consider it from two perspectives: one of internal origin, considering the attributes (strengths) of the organization or individuals; and the other from external origin, being the attributes of the environment. Looking at these areas and considering strengths, weaknesses, opportunities, and threats, helps all stakeholders self-analyze their possible products and services. Encouraging students to use this process to analyze their prototypes and ideas and to assess their strengths and weaknesses places them in the same framework of analysis used in the real world. This has a greater impact than creating a fun activity for a simulation of a business scenario to be used in the classroom.

Involve Students in Assessing the Process as Well as the Product

Chloe Maxmin has an intrinsic motivation to continually change, grow, and reevaluate her ventures. Without teacher direction and a formal process, she continually assesses her current success with her desired goals and potential influence. She rethinks her products and services and involvement and aligns her learning experiences to help reach her goals. When she graduated from high school, she traveled to South America and China where she studied prevalent environmental issues in both regions before heading to Harvard. This shows her desire to learn more about the global issues leading to climate change—she took a proactive role in learning what she wanted and needed in her learner-driven mode of knowledge acquisition.

Using product-oriented learning in a model that also promotes student autonomy and personalized learning, this mindset of self-assessing is what we want all students to embrace—to learn how to do it and why to do it. In a school setting, the process needs to be facilitated and documented, but students should have the tools and develop the skills necessary to complete the assessment on an "as needed" basis to drive their next steps. They need to be able to not only evaluate their product, but evaluate the steps they are taking in the process.

Following is a rubric created for inquiry that will lead to a product or service as the solution to a real-world need. The rubric is process oriented as it is connected to the steps of POL (product-oriented learning), but references the product or service so that both can be evaluated at once. It may be used to assess the various steps of the process and as a reflective tool to drive student goal setting and the creation of an action plan for success. This idea can be adjusted and simplified for younger students, but it is important to make sure the process is connected to the product.

Product-Oriented Learning Rubric: Inquiry Leading to a Product or Service

	Ineffective	Partially Effective	Effective	Highly Effective
	Limited inquiry and problem solving resulted in the inability to create a needed product or service.	Inquiry and some problem solving resulted in a product/service for a current real world need and is presented to an audience.	Relevant inquiry and strong problem-solving abilities resulted in an innovative product or service for a current real-world need and is marketed to an authentic customer.	Rigorous and relevant inquiry resulted in divergent thinking and the creation of multiple solutions to a current real-world need. An innovative product or service was created and successfully marketed on a global stage to authentic customers.
Use Inquiry to Identify a Need Based on Current Issues	Student did not embrace opportunities to impact positive change with current unsolved problems, unsatisfying conditions, or unmet needs.	Student was open to opportunities to impact positive change with current unsolved problems, unsatisfying conditions, or unmet needs.	Student was alert, curious about opportunities, and wanted to impact positive change with current unsolved problems, unsatisfying conditions, or unmet needs.	Student actively sought out multiple opportunities to impact positive change with current unsolved problems, unsatisfying conditions, or unmet needs.

(Continued)

45

(Continued)

	Ineffective	Partially Effective	Effective	Highly Effective
Generate Ideas	Student research was limited and did not result in an idea for a product or service.	Student engaged in research resulting in an idea for a product or service.	Student research was based on good questioning and resulted in multiple ideas for a product or service.	Student research was based on good questioning and divergent thinking and resulted in multiple innovative ideas by exploring many possible solutions.
Assess Strengths and Resources	Student was unable to analyze solutions for a product or service, or identify personal strengths and collaborative opportunities.	Student, with guidance, analyzed solutions to assess the capacity and resources to move forward with the product or service and identified personal strengths and opportunities for collaborative efforts.	Student analyzed solutions to assess the capacity and resources to move forward with the product or service and identified personal strengths and opportunities for collaborative efforts.	Student analyzed multiple solutions and created an in-depth assessment of the capacity and resources to create the product or service, identified personal strengths, and sought out opportunities for collaborative efforts.

	Ineffective	Partially Effective	Effective	Highly Effective
Convince Others	Student was unable to "sell" a product or service. A presentation for a product or service was not made.	Student presented a product to others within the school. A public presentation was used to showcase a product/service to others.	Student "sold" an innovative idea both in and outside the school. A business plan or public presentation was used to showcase that the product/service meets significant needs, is feasible and valuable, and that someone will buy or benefit from it.	Student "sold" an innovative idea to an intended audience. A business plan or public presentation was used to defend the product/ service in depth and convince others that it meets significant needs, is feasible and valuable, and that someone will buy or benefit from it.
Make the Product or Service	Student was not involved in creating a product or service. Product or service was not created.	Student worked individually or as a member of a team on the product or service. Product or service reflects little evidence of multiple drafts, critiques, peer reviews and revisions.	Student worked individually or as a member of a team on the product or service. Product or service reflects evidence of multiple drafts, critiques, peer reviews and revisions.	Student worked individually or on a team with real-world experts on the product or service. Product or service reflects evidence of multiple drafts, critiques, peer reviews and revisions, as well as feedback from real world experts.

(Continued)

	Ineffective	Partially Effective	Effective	Highly Effective
Market the Product	Student was unable to market a product or service.	Student marketed a product or service to a general audience.	Student employed marketing skills and tools within a medium and venue to sell the product or service to the intended customer.	Student employed various marketing skills and tools within a variety of media and venues to sell the product or service to the intended customer.
	Entrepreneurial competencies of reflection, resilience, confidence, communication, & perseverance were lacking.	Only a few of the following entrepreneurial competencies were evident: reflection, resilience, confidence, communication, & perseverance.	The entrepreneurial competencies of reflection, resilience, confidence, communication, and perseverance were evident.	The entrepreneurial competencies of reflection, resilience, confidence, communication, and perseverance were used to optimize marketing successes.
Manage and Maintain the Product or Service	NA	Student shows some involvement in the product-oriented learning cycle with limited engagement in managing sales, maintaining product or service, and communicating with users/customers.	Student continues on the product-oriented learning cycle and manages sales, maintains/upgrades product or service, and communicates with users/customers.	Student demonstrates an entrepreneurial mindset as he or she manages and promotes sales to a global market, maintains/upgrades the product or service, and communicates with users/customers on a regular basis.

Created by Kay Tucker (http://goo.gl/ciWcsN)

Involve Real-World Experts
in the Review and Assessment Process

Many people have benefitted from Chloe's ventures and many have contributed to her cause. She had a real-world audience from the beginning and received input from experts in the form of government officials, school administrators, interviewers, peers, community members, and possibly, land developers. In the classroom setting, the process of product-oriented learning can seem more contrived, but if the process stems from curiosity and students find problems in the world they are passionate about solving, it makes the task of connecting students to experts easier. In fact, many times the students are able to suggest ideas for the specific expert, or kind of expert, they want to have review their ideas.

If students do not know of an expert they can connect with, it is the role of the teacher to make sure that students find some avenue to connect with adults in the process of review and revision. The feedback is crucial and elevates the process of creating a feasible product or service to a level beyond the scope of a classroom assignment. It is this reality check that will spur students on to revise and perfect their product in the hopes that it will be not only needed, but also usable.

Whether teachers help create a one-to-one connection for a specific student's project, or bring in a panel of experts to provide feedback for a number of students, the process is invaluable. One example is a group of sixth-grade students who want to build a bridge behind their school, making it easier for the students to access their neighborhood. They created a proposal and a design, and presented their ideas to many experts including city officials and local recreation departments who oversee open space. The feedback they received, which included an astronomical price tag, forced them to rethink the project. The team of sixth graders researched and interviewed more adults, and found out that they could redesign a trail for less money, but still have a positive impact on making their community more accessible. They went on to organize a meeting with a school district employee in charge of operations who was very encouraging about the possibility of the trail being constructed. Had the students never engaged in conversation with these adult experts, they would have left the project unfinished, with beautiful designs, and no realistic application or use. In traditional models, this unrealistic design may have satisfied an assignment requirement and warranted a good grade. In this entrepreneurial model, however, the learning and application was much deeper and the students created a realistic product with the help and guidance of adults.

STRATEGIES FOR PRODUCING QUALITY PRODUCTS

In the Classroom

Create a Climate and Culture for Review and Revision

(See Activity #3: Create Strategies for Successful Review/Revision Processes)

When setting the culture for "making as learning" in our classrooms, it is important to allow for the time and repetition it takes to create a feasible product or service. Depending on the age of the student, the specific educational situation, and the comfort level of the teacher, the strategies and systems created will look different. The main idea is to allow students to create and test more than one idea. They should then share their idea to their peers for review and have the time to revise and reflect on their revisions. After feedback from real-world experts, the revision process may happen again. The resilience to persevere through this process so that a quality product is created should be central to everyday activities in the classroom.

Put Systems in Place for Students
to Choose Appropriate Tools for Assessment

Once again, as the aim in this model is to cultivate the entrepreneurial spirit and skills of students, using tools that are used in the workforce is a viable action. Have these tools available in your classroom and educate students as to their value. Model how to use them and suggest when appropriate that a student or team of students may be ready to "SWOT it out" to further analyze their ideas. Especially when students get stuck or have a hard time staying on task with their action plan, that is the time to work with them on setting SMART goals.

Make Self-Evaluation and Goal Setting a Common Practice

As fundamental as reading, writing, and math is the ability to set goals and be able to reflect and self-evaluate. Many times this is thought of as an adult skill, but this skill is crucial for students when scripting their own learning pathways and when designing real-world projects. Our discussions and expectations should include students including time for this as part of their learning pathway. For younger students, this could be part of the conversation— "Let's look at how we can set a goal together based on how you rate yourself."

In the School

Create Greater Opportunities
for Connecting to Real-World Experts

Surveys can be done on the school level to obtain data about the strengths, passions, and professions of your major stakeholders. Reach out to businesses in your community, large or small. Lone Tree Elementary is connecting with Charles Schwab, who has a large campus near the school, in an effort to build community, provide students with mentors, as well as expand the knowledge base of personal financial literacy for their students. Charles Schwab organizes a volunteer week every year in May when their volunteering "schwabbies" head out on service projects to benefit their greater community. They will connect with students in Lone Tree for multiple reasons: to help in the community garden at the school, to provide panels of experts that students will interview, and to be available to review student projects. This one connection opened the door for discussions about collaborative efforts beyond the designated week a year to many possibilities across the year based on students' needs.

Work with Parents to Align the Thinking in Your Building

Jackie Insinger, Insinger Insights, talks about the importance of parents working with their children to create SMART goals at home.

> Goal setting is a life skill and is key in discovering what motivates each child. When kids set goals, they feel empowered with choice, and they become emotionally involved. We set goals as a family and course-correct as needed—if off-track, it is always important to do this. (Insinger, 2015)

Her message is a simple message to parents—start small, but start! If setting goals is the same at home as it is at school, students begin to understand the steps and value of the process.

In the School System

Lead Systemic Thinking for Processes
Leading to Self-Assessment, Review, and Revision

The focus of a school system is often on mandated tests and tests that monitor progress using standardized methods across a school year. Setting similar importance on student self-assessment leading to goal setting and the valuable processes of review and revision could lead to a much-needed change in thinking as to how and what we assess in education. Starting these conversations at the higher levels of education could have a greater impact than hoping to have the change occur based on classroom and school-level efforts.

Make Visible the Strengths,
Passions, and Areas of Expertise of Employees

As in the case with a district expert embracing the opportunity to work alongside sixth graders working to build a new path between their school and their community, experts in district or school systems can be an invaluable resource to our students. Make this a visible and viable option. Consider including in a Staff Directory, areas of strengths and passions alongside area of professional expertise, so that students could contact employees for occasional guidance and feedback to help them in the process of review and revision.

OVERCOMING CHALLENGES

Changing how and what we assess is crucial when we change our instructional models to ones of innovation. For too long we have assessed isolated chunks of content and skills separated into a scope and sequence based on age. To continue this kind of assessment does nothing to empower students with the integrated approach to real-world learning that is needed. We need to begin using and promoting an integrated approach to the assessment of processes and products. Students' passions and strengths should direct their learning and lead them to creative and worthwhile endeavors. We need to give students ample time and flexibility in a school setting to do this—come up with ideas to solve problems, create, revise, "sell" the product or service, market and maintain it. For that amount of time, we also need to make sure we support and assess both the processes involved and the content that is uncovered as a student-driven curriculum. In the entrepreneurship model, we should be supporting and assessing what students love and changing our traditional methods to meet the needs of this approach. Chloe Maxmin is evidence that this approach works.

ACTIVITY #1: GET SMART!

Participants: Teachers, students, school administrative teams, or district-level educators

Objective: SMART goals may be used to drive success in a business (product or service), or to achieve a personal goal. Both of these come into play when considering students developing skills alongside a product. Aligning product development with personal development promotes success in both areas. Participants will brainstorm and examine ways to use this strategy as an effective tool with their staff or students.

Materials

- Note-taking material—digital devices or chart paper, markers

Organization: Partners

Process

Review SMART goals and example in the "Help students create SMART goals" section on page 42. (5–10 minutes)

Discuss the important components of setting a SMART goal.

Discuss how this process was used in the example and how it could be used for self-evaluation and targeted results in learning as well as product development.

Create a sample SMART goal and analyze. (20 minutes)

- Consider
  - ○ A possible scenario for a student creating a product or service.
  - ○ An example from your current situation where a SMART goal could impact progress and change.

- Analyze the possible outcomes for setting these goals.
- Discuss a possible framework for managing student SMART goals.

Share your example and thinking with another group. (20 minutes)

- List any similarities in thinking between the two groups.
- Identify any revelations of new thinking.

Reflection: (10 minutes) Share out any new take-aways or possibilities for this strategy.

Next Steps

After using this strategy in the classroom, reflect on these questions:

- How has the implementation of SMART goals for students impacted student-driven learning pathways and projects?
- Did this process influence the process of review and revision leading to a quality product?

ACTIVITY #2: SWOT IT OUT!

Participants: Teachers, students, school administrative teams, or district-level educators

Objective: When organizations consider whether or not a venture will be feasible, they evaluate the product or service using strategies such as the SWOT analysis (Strengths, Weaknesses, Opportunities, and Threats). They consider it from two perspectives: one of internal origin, considering the attributes (strengths) of the organization or individuals, and the other from external origin, being the attributes of the environment. Looking at these areas and considering strengths, weaknesses, opportunities, and threats will help all stakeholders self-analyze their possible products and services.

Following graphic is from http://commons.wikimedia .org/wiki/File:SWOT_en.svg#filelinks

SWOT ANALYSIS		
	Helpful to achieving the objective	**Harmful** to achieving the objective
Internal origin (attributes of the organization)	**Strengths** (S)	**Weaknesses** (W)
External origin (attributes of the environment)	**Opportunities** (O)	**Threats** (T)

Materials

- Digital devices
- Copies of SWOT chart
- Chart paper
- Markers

Organization: Groups of four to six

Process

Google SWOT (10 minutes)

Discuss definitions and develop an understanding of the process and how it is used.

Business at School (15 minutes)

Use the chart paper to document how the SWOT approach applies in a school setting using product-oriented learning.

Roleplay (20 minutes)

Group yourselves as follows:

- One student presenting one idea to one teacher or mentor
- Two to three students presenting one idea to one teacher or mentor
- Two to three students presenting one idea to a pair of adults (teachers and mentors)

Student(s): Present an idea for a product or service to the teacher(s).

Teacher/Mentor: Use the SWOT strategy to drive a discussion that helps the student(s) self-analyze their product or service.

Reflection: (10 minutes)

- Did this process help drive a dialogue about the potential for a product or service?
- Were the students able to determine next steps based on the discussion?

Next Steps

After using this strategy in the classroom, reflect on these questions:

- Has using the SWOT analysis helped bring a sense of reality to the many possible ideas generated by students? If so, how?
- Did this process positively redirect and aid in the process of review and revision?

ACTIVITY #3: CREATE STRATEGIES FOR SUCCESSFUL REVIEW AND REVISION PROCESSES

Participants: Teachers, students, school administrative teams, or district-level educators

Objective: In product-oriented learning, one of the most important processes for students is the actual making of the product or service. It should reflect evidence of multiple drafts, critiques, peer reviews, and revisions, as well as feedback from real-world experts. This is also the area where teachers struggle the most as it is a commitment of time and seemingly repetitive efforts. It is where students may fail and want to give up, but where they need to persevere. This activity will help educators look at the challenges of the process of review and revision and brainstorm ways to manage this valuable cyclical process leading to a quality product.

Materials

- Chart paper and markers
- Three colors of Post-It notes—yellow, blue, green (or a workable substitute)

Organization:

Various groupings

Areas established in room for posting notes

- Area 1—divided into
  - Teacher challenges
  - Teacher solution

- Area 2—divided into
  - Student challenges
  - Student solutions

Process

Challenges (10 minutes)

In groups of four to six, discuss the challenges of this process.

- Consider the challenges of the teacher and write on yellow Post-It notes.
- Consider the challenges of the students and write on blue Post-It notes.

Post notes in the designated area of the room. One area should be designated for teachers/yellow, and one area for students/blue.

What do the challenges have in common? (10 minutes)

Divide the group in half to analyze the challenges and group them by common themes. Once they have been grouped, add titles to the groupings essentially creating a category.

- One half analyzes, groups, and titles the teacher challenges.
- One half analyzes, groups, and titles the student challenges.

Ideate solutions to the perceived challenges. (15 minutes)

Participants will choose a category and team up to ideate solutions, or strategies to use, that address the challenges. Make sure every category has a solutions team.
Each solutions team will

- Consider the challenges of their category;
- Generate multiple ideas as possible solutions;
- Write two to three main solutions on the green Post-It notes and post on the solutions chart next to the challenges chart—either teacher or student.

What do the solutions have in common? (5 minutes)

Return to analyze the solutions and group and title them by commonalities.

Groups switch to view and discuss the visible thinking. (10 minutes)

Reflection: (10 minutes)

Return to large group to share findings and reflections about how these solutions could be implemented as strategies in your classroom or school.

Next Steps

After being back in the classroom or school, reflect on the following:

- If you were able to incorporate any of the generated solutions to the challenges, reflect on their effectiveness.
- How does having systems in place for the review and revision process add value to the student learning process?

REFERENCES

Big Ideas for a Small Planet—Communities. (n.d.). Retrieved March 20, 2015, from http://www.sundance.tv/videos/communities-big-ideas-for-a-small-planet-season-3-episode-11-clip

Elias, M. (2014, August 27). SMART goal setting with your students. *Edutopia.* Retrieved from http://www.edutopia.org/blog/smart-goal-setting-with-students-maurice-elias

First Here, Then Everywhere. (n.d.). Retrieved on June 5, 2015, from http://firsthereneverywhere.org

Insinger, J. (2015). Personal communication.

Maxmin, C. (2015). About FHTE. Retrieved on June 5, 2015, from http://firsthereneverywhere.org/about/about-fhte/

NoTosh. (n.d.). Retrieved June 5, 2015, from http://notosh.com/what-we-do/the-design-thinking-school/

SMART criteria. (2015, June 6). In *Wikipedia, The Free Encyclopedia.* Retrieved June 5, 2015, from http://en.wikipedia.org/w/index.php?title=SMART_criteria&oldid=665811158

SWOT analysis. (2015, May 21). In *Wikipedia, The Free Encyclopedia.* Retrieved June 7, 2015, from http://en.wikipedia.org/w/index.php?title=SWOT_analysis&oldid=663375012

Zhao, Y. (2012). *World class learners: Educating creative and entrepreneurial students.* Thousand Oaks, CA: Corwin.

4

Making as Learning

Product-Oriented Learning and Curriculum Standards

by Kay Tucker

"In school, you're taught a lesson and then given a test. In life, you're given a test that teaches you a lesson."

—Tom Bodett

"In a World Class School, students should have certain degrees of freedom to pursue their own interests. Thus schools must have a broad range of curriculum offerings and flexible range to enable students to explore, experience, and experiment with their interests and passions."

—Zhao (2012, pp. 245–246)

Featured School

St. Paul's School, Queensland, Australia

St. Paul's School, Queensland, Australia, has a team of educators committed to creating an environment for learning that is student centered, passion based, and learner driven—where students can discover their gifts and talents without a fear of failure. Their aim is to prepare students to be contributing global citizens, starting with a strong sense of empathy. Education at St. Paul's School is relevant and empowering. "Create your own story!" (St. Paul's School, 2014) is not only the tagline on their website, but it encapsulates the fundamental quality of the school as students are encouraged to follow their interests and passions as they script and live out their individual stories.

The educators at St. Paul's are also actively pursuing the question, "What is an education worth having?" They are being recognized as leaders because of their work in the development of learning that is real and relevant. The school was selected by the Australian Institute of Teachers and School Leaders (AITSL) to be a Lab Site (design hub) for Learning Frontiers. "Learning Frontiers is a collaborative initiative created to transform teaching and learning so that every student succeeds in an education worth having" (Australian Institute of Teachers and School Leaders, 2014). The purpose of the program is to bring together groups of schools in order to explore professional practices that will increase the level of student engagement in learning. Within the four design principles of engaging learning—co-created, personal, connected, integrated—"design hubs" (Lab Sites) explore practices related to teaching, learning, and assessments.

Combining the school's mission and vision with the challenge of being a design hub for Learning Frontiers, a team of teachers found inspiration for an engaging and relevant student learning project from a real-life example found in Vancouver, Canada. The inspiration was a collaborative effort between Atira Women's Resource Society, Canada Mortgage, and Housing Corporation, BC Hydro, and other community partners. This partnership created Canada's first recycled shipping container social housing development that was cost-effective, met a real-world need by providing much needed affordable housing, was sustainable using an environmentally sensitive building option, and served to bridge communities. Executive Director of Teaching and Learning at St. Paul's School, Jon Andrews, writes about how this successful project in Canada led teacher leaders to question: "So what can school students learn from unique social ventures like this? Can students deeply engage themselves in a project which would be design led, encourage entrepreneurial talent to surface and connect them through service learning to community needs?" (Andrews, 2014).

The answer to the last question was yes, and the Community Pathways Project (CPP) at St. Paul's School was created. The school project was designed around the same ideas that made the real-world project stand out as a motivational and strong guiding example. The project addresses each of the four defining principles defined by Learning Frontiers. It will be **co-created** by students and mentors and will seek to involve community partners and will be highly **personal** as it harnesses specific talents and interests of the students. The project work will be **connected** to real-world scenarios with a social entrepreneurship focus where students can practice empathy and also make connections to what is important in their own lives. Finally, it has the natural **integration** of subject areas and professional skills such as collaboration, problem finding and solving, effective communication, and decision making. Jon Andrews accurately qualifies this project by saying, "With a service focus, this is authentically work that matters" (Andrews, 2014). Where the structure will be located and which greater community it will serve may not yet be decided, but when decisions are made, the students will make them. Whether the structure is funded and finally completed, is not as important to the staff of St. Paul's School as the valuable processes that all of the students will go through in this personalized approach to engaging learning.

We want our students to do work that matters and to be able to generate ideas based on real-world needs. We want them to have empathy and to explore, experience, and experiment—to learn as they design and create viable products or services. The Community Pathways Project as envisioned by St. Paul's School is an approach to learning that engages students in all of these aspects very successfully and exemplifies the idea of making for learning in a model for product-oriented learning.

PRINCIPLES OF MAKING AS LEARNING, UNCOVERING THE STANDARDS

- POL (product-oriented learning) addresses the "Relevance and Application" aspects of standards.
- Facilitating POL within a context allows students to uncover the standards.
- POL allows learners to be creators instead of consumers.
- Entrepreneurism and POL integrate real-world curriculum.

POL Addresses the "Relevance and Application" Aspect of Standards

There are many aspects of standards-based learning. Once a standard is determined, it is deconstructed and prescribed as a scope and sequence across all grade levels, finally leading to graduate-level understanding. Within each grade level, there is a set of outcomes that students should be able to perform during the course of a school year. As well as outcomes, there are descriptors of relevance and application— how this standard is relevant and applicable in real-world scenarios. This is the valuable realm where product-oriented learning resides. It is the reality of noncompartmentalized learning where the standard connects with other standards to create meaning.

The integrated and connected approach that can be applied in the Community Pathways Project exemplifies how students naturally address "standards learning." Instead of forcing content to be connected—as is the idea with applied academics where students learn first in a classroom and then cement their learning via internships, service learning, etc.— POL starts with the real-world connection and students uncover standards that are relevant to the project. As students plan to repurpose a shipping container, it is necessary to learn aspects of design and computer technologies before they can be successful in others aspects of the product creation.

Traditional subject boundaries are replaced with a "coming-together of the disciplines with a project focus." The learning is just-in-time and allows students to apply knowledge and skills in an ongoing, meaningful, and deep manner. As Jon Andrews stated, "The mobility of these skills will be critical in an uncertain future, but to be able to develop a portfolio of practice that exemplifies critical fluencies, is a great outcome" (Andrews, 2014).

Facilitating POL Within Context
Allows Students to Uncover the Standards

(See Activity #2: We Are Aware, We Care, We Prepare, We Share)

The key to success in a product-oriented learning model is changing the role of the teacher to one of a facilitator. This shifts the purpose of a teacher to "one who allows students to uncover the curriculum" as opposed to "one who needs to cover the curriculum." Allowing students to "uncover" within a context for learning drives valuable discussion and inquiry around the very content areas educators are responsible to teach. At Lone Tree Elementary (LTE), Colorado, teachers took part in a professional development course I designed specifically to frame the process of, and provide resources for, product-oriented learning. I created the table "The Roles of Students and Teachers in Product-Oriented Learning" as a tool to specifically draw attention to the facilitative role of teachers in this process. The staff used it to align specific instructional strategies to the related student activities for each essential step in the process of product-oriented learning. Teachers shifted their roles from a teacher-directed paradigm to a learner-driven paradigm as they led their students through this process that was personalized within a context for learning. The steps in the table are an adaptation of the steps involved in the process of product-oriented learning written about by Yong Zhao in *World Class Learners* (2012, p. 204).

Table 4.1   The Roles of Students and Teachers in Product-Oriented Learning

Steps in the Process	Roles of Students	Roles of Teachers
Identify Needs	Students are alert, curious to opportunities, and want to impact positive change with unsolved problems, unsatisfying conditions, or unmet needs.	Teachers replace the obstacles of "content-driven education" with a context in which students can find entrepreneurial opportunities. They cultivate students who are curious, empathetic to others, and see problems as opportunities to create positive change.
Generate Ideas	Students engage in research and creative problem-solving processes resulting in a possible product or service.	Teachers create context, organize brainstorming sessions, facilitate the process, provide resources and connections to experts, and make suggestions.
Assess Strengths and Weaknesses	Students analyze their solution to assess whether they have the capacity and resources to move forward. They identify their own strengths and understand it is not what they can do alone, but what they can learn to do with the help of others.	Teachers provide students the opportunity to identify and further enhance their strengths while avoiding weaknesses. They may suggest "outsourcing" as a way of partnering, as we are not all equally good at everything and have different levels of strengths and weaknesses.
Convince Someone	Students need to convince others that the needs they are meeting are significant, the proposed product or service is of value and is feasible, and that someone will buy or benefit from the product or service. Business plans or public presentations	Teachers serve many roles: *Venture capitalist* helps decide if the project is needed and feasible. *Consultant* provides suggestions and resources.

Steps in the Process	Roles of Students	Roles of Teachers
	to "sell" their ideas should be presented in and outside the school. Multiple drafts, critiques, peer reviews, and revisions come into play as their plan may not be accepted initially.	*Motivator* encourages at times of disappointment. *Focus Group* provides feedback and critique on prototype. *Partner* provides complementary expertise and skills.
Make the Product/ Service	Students work individually or in teams on approved product or service. Once again multiple drafts, critiques, peer reviews, and revisions come into play.	Teachers connect students with professionals as reviewers and mentors to raise standard of product/service.
Market the Product/ Service	Students learn marketing skills and tools as they use a variety of media and venues to sell their product or service to the intended customer. They develop the entrepreneurial competencies of reflection, resilience, confidence, communication, and perseverance.	Teachers engage professionals or community members as mentors for their students and suggest applicable marketing strategies.
Post-Product Management and Maintenance	Students continue on the product-oriented learning cycle and they manage sales (online or other), maintain and upgrade the product or service, and communicate with users and customers.	Teachers continue to provide feedback and offer suggestions and resources.

For sixth grade at LTE, their context for learning was based on the statement: "The world is in our hands." As they analyzed the cause and effect of global issues (deforestation, fracking, erosion, ice caps, climate change, pollution, etc.) and answered the question, "How do our decisions impact physical systems?" they developed multiple ideas for products and services. This approach allowed students to go beyond the understanding of a curriculum standard. The application and relevancy of the standards came to life with the authentic products and services created using the product-oriented learning process. All of the teachers recognized that what their students learned could not be quantified, and went beyond a set purpose for instruction and intended learning goals. The result of shifting roles as a teacher to one of a facilitator allowed the students to uncover curriculum standards and the teachers were successful in facilitating deep and personal learning. They planted the seed for entrepreneurial thinking.

POL Allows Learners to Be Creators Instead of Consumers

The famous quote by Gandhi, "Be the change you want to see in the world" headlines the website created for the iLab Capstone Project for seventh-grade students at Mountain Ridge Middle School in Douglas County, Colorado. This project challenges students to use Design Thinking as the process to create solutions to problems and is framed as an opportunity to, "[T]ake something that inspires you and to make a difference. This is your choice and voice!" (iLab Capstone Project, 2014).

Students are first asked to consider what makes them curious and what inspires them. Using an inquiry process, they identify a problem or need, and then brainstorm and generate ideas for multiple solutions to the problem. After evaluating the possibilities, students develop one innovative way to approach solving the problem. Carrying out their plans or designs, they create the products or services, implement the solutions and then carry out the plans.

Speaking from personal strengths and authentic interests, the students crafted an incredible array of questions based on pertinent real world issues. Here are a few:

- How can I create a program and environment that makes students open up to their past and create an even better future?
- How can I create a reliable, cheap, and effective way to reuse water in schools?
- How can I use art therapy to help reduce the depression rate in Colorado?
- How can we reduce the environmental effects of a ski resort?

It is easy to see the connections that these questions have to content standards. As the students research in order to be creative problem solvers, they dig deep into science, civics, and economics, as well as develop skills for oral and written communication, and other 21st century skills. When they connect their role in the world to these important issues, and are given a voice, it is easy to see their passion and excitement grow. Excitement generates engagement and engagement is the driving force behind the breadth of curriculum that a student will uncover on his or her own. Instead of consuming information created by someone else, they are building understanding as they create information for others. When asked about the content in iLab, one of the teachers, Russell Loucks, responds:

> The simple answer is . . . a student's passion and curiosity. iLab, like math and language arts, is a skills class. Students have the opportunity to learn the skills necessary to be successful in consuming a large amount of information (critical thinking), creating solutions and products to combat real-world problems in teams (collaboration & problem solving), and delivering their solutions with digital tools (communication). (Loucks, 2014)

Entrepreneurism and POL Integrate Real-World Curriculum

There is no doubt that product-oriented learning will prepare our students to function as professionals in a modern world.

It presents opportunities for students to make connections to their communities with pervasive themes: environment, resources, economies, cultural connections, human needs, and technologies. These themes are constantly changing, are opportunities for action, and are the basis for many curriculum standards. If done with fidelity, product-oriented learning ultimately results in the following.

- Rigorous and relevant inquiry resulting in divergent thinking and the creation of multiple solutions to a current real world need
- An innovative product or service that is created and successfully marketed on a global stage to authentic customers

Entrepreneurs solve problems for others and create products and services that meet real-world needs, and this way of thinking is now being considered as a key component in preparing students for future success. Focusing on creating responsible citizens who can visualize what can be done to meet a real-world need, and then go about doing what it takes to make it happen, is the basis of product-oriented learning. It is rooted in real-life with modern day situations sparking curiosity. This curiosity then takes the form of action-inquiry where student-generated questions drive a process of critical thinking, creativity, and design, in order to solve problems. The broad outcome is that students will create solutions to current real-world needs and these solutions will be in the form of a product or service.

The entrepreneurial focus of the Community Pathways Project at St. Paul's School is obvious with the student outcomes rich in multiple content areas and in the application of 21st century skills. The real-world challenge prompted critical thinking across multiple content areas. Focused on a common task, the students combined their personal strengths and passions to create unique solutions to a real-world problem. Using a design thinking process the students engaged in a collaborative effort to potentially impact positive change in a greater community.

Strategies for Making as Learning, Uncovering the Standards

In the Classroom

Develop Common Language and Understanding

Spend time establishing an understanding of what it means to be an entrepreneur, a social entrepreneur, or an organizational entrepreneur. Develop rich vocabulary and common language related to entrepreneurial thinking and the steps of product-oriented learning. Create opportunities for a "Mystery Entrepreneurs" activity or Skype/Hangout with entrepreneurs allowing students to engage in interviews and ask their own questions. For examples of more easy things to try, refer to Lisa Chesser's blog titled "50 Ideas to Bring Entrepreneurship to the Classroom," where she affirms,

> Teaching kids about startups and small business inside a classroom not only meets any set of standards, it prepares them for life. Students learn about brainstorming ideas, setting goals, budgeting, and indulging their individuality while still learning to cooperate with others. (Chesser, 2013)

Authentically Assess Students Within a Context for Learning

(See Activity #1: Are these assessments for real?)

Refresh one unit of study to be interest-driven inquiry within a context for learning that results in an authentic performance assessment. To be authentic, it needs to be used in a real-world situation or have a real-world audience. This stipulation alone increases the boundaries of curriculum and drives real-world activities. Below are some examples of performance assessments related to creating a business with a product or service. Give students the opportunity to present these to authentic audiences and allow them time to revise based on the feedback given. These steps can lead to creative and entrepreneurial thinking and maybe an actual product or service to be marketed.

Table 4.2   Performance Tasks Leading to a Product or Service

Testing	Proposing	Gathering Feedback	Assessing and Organizing	Marketing and Promoting
Experiments	Animation	Blog	Budget analysis	Advertisement
Journals	Artist rendering	Demonstration	Flowchart	Billboards
Observation		#hashtag	Fundraiser	Branding ideas
b(log)	Blueprint	Letter	Seed funds	Brochures
Opinion polls	Diagram	Opinion poll		Editorials
Photo journals	Field guide	Survey		Event planning
Research study	Midel	Twitter feed		Graphics
Science journal	Position paper	Website		Infographics
Scientific process surveys	Prototype			Infomercials
	Scale drawing			Logo creation
	Scientific drawing			Menu design
	Virtual walk through			Newscast
				Photostory
				Press release
				Sales pitch
				TedTalk
				Twitter
				Website

Actively Involve Families in the POL Process

Entrepreneurism and product-oriented learning comes alive in third grade at Lone Tree Elementary School. After establishing the definition of an entrepreneur and going through the initial process of product-oriented learning, the students determined a need in their school community for which they wanted to create a solution. This need was that students wanted to be able to shop and buy items for their families during the holiday season in a manner that was more independent than being driven to the mall and supervised by adults. Their solution was to organize an event for the community to be held mid-December that would sell items that were both appealing and yet affordable for students. One group of students became the event planners—finding the place to hold the event, selling spaces to those who wanted to sell at the event, and advertising the event. Other students joined together in small groups to create small businesses that created sellable products. The students found adult mentors to guide them through the process of creating a viable product or service, as well as the steps to understand what makes a business successful and profitable. These adults guided the students as they refined their products and established a price in order to generate enough profit to rent their booth and cover costs. Excitement throughout the parent community grew with the realization of how great an experience this was for the students—an experience that gave them the foundation in order to branch out and apply these same skills as they create other real-world solutions in the future. This involvement alone solidified the value of this approach to learning in the minds of a large population of stakeholders in the building.

Connect Globally and Expand
Opportunities Aligned to your Curriculum

As well as opening up your curriculum through POL for personalized learning for individual students, engage your entire class in a service learning initiative that aligns with your curriculum. Go beyond your classroom and investigate real-world problems related to combined science and/ or social studies' standards and find the context that excites and engages students. Inspire students to take action based on real-world needs and use these ideas to create a business for your class to run.

Anne Malamud teaches a 4/5 class at Mills College Children's School, the laboratory school for the School of Education at Mills College in Oakland, California. Originally her class embarked on what might be called a civic-minded or responsible citizen project with the goal of raising money for a nonprofit organization. Their venture, named the Happy Eating Place, started with the main intent of preparing healthy snacks, but has grown to include educating others to the importance of sustainable farming and the causes of hunger in America. Malamud inspired her students by looking beyond the classroom, giving all students a stake in the business, and allowing them to fail in the learning process. These strategies combined as valuable lessons as well as addressed many areas of standardized curriculum (social studies and social justice, civics, math, life science, writing)—all in an entrepreneurial approach to a service-learning project.

Read more about this social learning project in the Edutopia blog written by Whitney Walker: "The Happy Eating Place: How Elementary Students Can Run Their Own Business" (Walker, 2014).

In the School

Increase Community Awareness
and Involve the Greater Community

Educate all stakeholders as to the purpose and relevance of making for learning and product-oriented learning: Create a web-based information and resource site; organize small group sessions for Q&As and how to get involved (PTO, SAC, parent coffees, etc.); host speaker sessions; actively involve families in the process.

Solicit help from community members to serve as mentors, consultants, and experts for students. These adults would be willing to help in the following processes:

- Evaluate and consult in the ongoing process of multiple drafts, critiques, peer reviews, and revisions.
- Provide real-world analysis and recommendations for youth products and ventures.
- Collaboratively assess, provide feedback, and set future goals for growth of model within school and greater community.

Create a Viable System With
POL as the Umbrella for all Learning

(See Activity #3: Action Timeline for "Making as Learning" Across the Years)

If individuals, schools, or systems are considering implementing "Making as Learning," or product-oriented learning, as a foundational approach, there should be a sequenced plan in place. What does this look like across all of the years in your school system or district? What should happen first? How do you grow the concepts, ideas, and experiences across the years? Having specific systems and expectations in place will not only guide staff through the process, but will guarantee experiences, common language, and a general approach to learning.

Create a Body of Evidence
for Product-Oriented Learning Across the Years

Begin early and be consistent with student inquiry and plant the seeds for enterprising youth with systems and tools in place.

- Have all students create online resumes as part of their digital portfolio.
- Teach the process of product-oriented learning and implement across all grade levels.
- Encourage younger grade levels to create a business as a class, going through the steps collaboratively.
- Actively teach students to create good questions beginning in kindergarten.
- Provide a forum for presentation of products within the school as a stepping stone to go global.

In the School System

Collaborate for Increased Opportunity

Collaborate with local businesses and government entities to provide increased opportunities for students. The Young

Entrepreneurs Academy (YEA!) is an after school program that works to transform middle and high school students into entrepreneurs. This collaborative effort between Douglas County Schools, Castle Rock Chamber of Commerce, and the Kauffman Foundation, guides middle and high school students through the process of starting and running a real business or social movement over the course of an academic year.

> YEA! students are taught to recognize the power of their ideas, and to turn those ideas into meaningful enterprises. Unlike the simulation models, at the end of the YEA! program, students own and operate fully formed and functioning businesses, which may be carried on by students after graduation. (Young Entrepreneurs Academy, n.d.)

What YEA! is doing as an after-school program could be taking place during the day and begin in younger grades. Create schools, charter, magnets or niche schools that have product-oriented learning as a model for learning across a K–12 environment.

Organize Event-Based Learning Opportunities

Create a memorable sense of occasion and spark new ideas and thinking with district-level or systemwide events. The possibilities and examples are endless, but the goal remains the same—to provide exciting opportunities in order to expand networks and to bring together a variety of voices and ideas. Events could be held for teachers and students separately or they could merge the realm of participants to include both for a variety of participation, engagement, and thinking. Organizing events that promote teams of teachers and students reinforces the sought after collaborative aspect between adults and students who co-create products or services. Ideas for events include:

- Inventfests
- Regional contests around any focus area (art, music, robotics, coding, etc)
- Maker-faire type events
- Entrepreneur hookups: Finding partners in business
- Think tanks

OVERCOMING CHALLENGES

It is impossible to separate curriculum standards from testing. In education today, they combine to be a driving force for what happens in classrooms. Within the realm of high-stakes testing and the reality of an established curriculum, teachers tend to work within the confines of what has proven to be "testworthy." While product-oriented learning gives teachers the framework for implementing a strong model for real-world inquiry, the automatic assumption is that doing something new, even if based on current needs, research, and best practices, will not give adequate results. It is also true that taking a risk to try something new only happens if there is a high-level of trust between stakeholders. One of our challenges is to ignore false assumptions and create levels of trust in order to implement innovative approaches to learning. When met with hesitancy to change instructional practice due to the demands of testing, Principal Mindy Persichina, coaches her teachers by saying: "Why would we be coaching you to do something new if we thought it would bring worse results? Take a risk—it is okay to fail, but let's keep moving forward!"

The results of all of the examples used in this chapter, where students are "making to learn," exceed the boundaries of a common curriculum. Students used critical thinking skills and applied their knowledge to pertinent situations. Consider the younger students who are creating healthy snacks for others and how they took their ideas beyond the classroom walls to impact a greater community. They could easily "check-off" a set of standards in doing so. Product-oriented learning is a best practices approach to learning—it moves the focus in education to prioritizing a real-world authentic assessment of learning and considers students' success as test-takers as a consequential secondary reward.

ACTIVITY #1: ARE THESE ASSESSMENTS FOR REAL?

Participants: Teachers, students, school administrative teams, or district-level educators

Objective: Assessing in a "making-for-learning" environment is what ties learning to standards-based progress reporting. In this activity, participants will make connections between real-world tasks and projects and possible authentic performance assessments to be used for reporting in a standards-based system.

Materials

- Copies of "Are These Assessments for Real?" (This table can be found online at http://bit.ly/1UyidRu.)
- Optional: Chart paper and markers for each group

Organization: Groups of two to three

Process (60 minutes)

Review/analyze performance assessments for product-oriented learning (10 minutes)

Refer to the section in this chapter under Classroom Strategies called: "Authentically assess students within a context for learning" (page 71)

   In a small group, analyze whether or not these are viable options for standards-based progress reporting.

- Which standards would these examples assess?
- Can you think of additional performance assessments for product-oriented learning?

Create and Assess (40 minutes)

- Use the template "Are these assessments for real?" or chart paper to complete this step.

- Come up with an idea for a sample product/service that could be created by a student, or group of students, within a context for learning.

- Review the steps that students will go through for product-oriented learning in the section of this chapter called: "Facilitating POL Within a Context Allows Students to Uncover the Standards" (see page 65).

- For each step in the process, list potential performance assessments from the chart on page 72.

- List the potential curriculum standards that would be addressed with these steps and assessments.

Are These Assessments for Real?

Come up with a sample product/service that could be created by a student(s) within a context for learning.

Product or Service:

For each step, list performance assessments and potential standards addressed.

Step in Process	Performance Assessment	Potential Standards Addressed
Identify Needs		
Generate Ideas		
Assess Strengths and Weaknesses		

(Continued)

(Continued)

Step in Process	Performance Assessment	Potential Standards Addressed
Convince Someone		
Make the Product/Service		
Market the Product/Service		
Post-Product Management and Maintenance		

Reflection: (10–20 minutes)

Participants rotate around the room (gallery walk) to view the ideas and analysis of other groups.

- What is the extent to which standards can be assessed if students go through the entire process of product-oriented learning?
- How does placing students within a context for learning help address required standards?
- Are there similarities in the standards across various performance standards?

Next Steps

After using this strategy in the classroom, reflect on these questions:

- How has connecting real-world type assessments impacted learning?
- How has this approach to assessments changed your thinking about assessments that have been assigned or utilized in the past?

Activity #2: We Are Aware, We Care, We Prepare, We Share

Participants: Teachers and students

Objective: We want students to do work that is important to them. At the same time, we need to be able to report on their mastery of outcomes. For each outcome, there are descriptors of its relevance and application in real world scenarios. It is this valuable realm that comes alive with product-oriented learning. Whether we choose to pick a focus from a broad range of topics or we are aligning learning within a context, this activity helps define what is important to learners in an interest-driven inquiry-based approach to uncovering standards.

Materials

- We Are Aware Chart (at https://goo.gl/m1ULJ3)

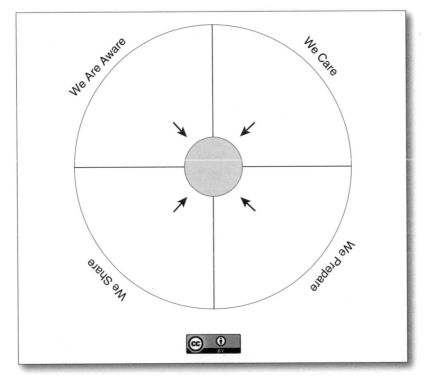

We Are Aware graphic by Kay Tucker is licensed under a Creative Commons Attribution 3.0 Unported License.

Organization: Complete activity as an individual. Partner share.

Process

Explain and complete the chart (30 minutes)

For this activity, we can consider something of personal interest from a broad spectrum, or we can consider what we find interesting within a contextual situation. The top half of the chart helps us to identify a need and to generate ideas for a product or service. The bottom half is where all of the making and implementing takes place. Complete the chart as follows to "center" your ideas on a focal point of interest in creating a product or service.

We are aware: To know what could be made as a possible product or service, we need to understand the world around us—to be aware of how it is changing and what needs are being created. *In this quadrant list some current real world happenings.* (Identify needs.)

We care: We have personal connections that make us care differently about happenings in the world. *In this quadrant list what it is you care about related to what is listed in the "We are aware" quadrant.* (Generate ideas.)

We prepare: Based on what you care about as listed in the previous quadrant, *what could you research, experiment with, and create to solve the problem you care about.* (Assess strengths, convince others, create a product or service.)

We share: Going back to the "We care" quadrant, who or what did you originally care about and define as a need? *How will you share or market your product or service to help solve the problem you cared about?* (Market the product or service, manage, and maintain.)

Reflection: (20 minutes)

Share with a partner how and why you completed the chart.

Why are you excited about the product or service you have chosen?

Does your focus align with a personal interest, strength, or passion?

Do you think it is possible to go through the entire process of product-oriented learning using this as an idea?

How will this focus allow you to create a learning pathway that will address assigned content?

Next Steps

After using this strategy in the classroom, reflect on these questions:

- What are the results of using this approach as the starting point of inquiry leading to a product or service?
- How would you change this activity to work better for your students?

ACTIVITY #3: ACTION TIMELINE FOR "MAKING AS LEARNING" ACROSS THE YEARS

Participants: Teachers, students, school administrative teams, or district-level educators

Objective: If individuals, schools, or systems are considering implementing "Making as Learning," or product-oriented learning, as a *foundational* approach, there should be a sequenced plan in place. What could this look like in your class, school or district? What should happen first? How do you grow the concepts, ideas, and experiences across the years? This activity will guide the thought process for planning that could lead to a viable system using product-oriented learning as the umbrella for all learning.

Materials

- Chart paper and markers, or
- Individual preference for charting and planning
- Digital tools (optional)

Organization: Group participants according to responsibility and range of grade levels (i.e., K–6, K–12, middle school, high school, etc.)

Process: (60 minutes total)

Review, Consider, Discuss (10 minutes)

Consider these suggestions for schools from the Strategies section of this chapter (page 75).

Begin early and be consistent with student inquiry and plant the seeds for enterprising youth with systems and tools in place.

- Have all students create online resumes as part of their digital portfolio.
- Teach the process of product-oriented learning and implement across all grade levels.
- Encourage younger grade levels to create a business as a class, going through the steps collaboratively.
- Actively teach students to create good questions beginning in kindergarten.
- Provide a forum for presentation of products within the school as a stepping stone to go global.

Create a timeline/plan (40 minutes)

Option 1: School or School System

Begin the timeline with your youngest age of students. For each age group think about how the experiences increase awareness of the process and the concepts within the process of product-oriented learning and how these connect to curriculum standards.

For example:

Kindergarten

- Experiences
- Concepts
- Connections to required content

Option 2: Classroom or one grade level
Timeline should span the school year. Begin at the start of the school year and end with your last month of teaching. Think about how the experiences increase awareness of the process and the concepts within the process of product-oriented learning and how these connect to curriculum standards.

First month

- Experiences
- Concepts
- Connections to required content

Reflection: (10 minutes)

Share big ideas or revelations with the larger group.

How does creating a plan like this increase the level of success for product-oriented learning?

How did the process of creating an action timeline expand your thinking of possibilities?

What are your thoughts on creating a common language and common experiences within a building and a larger community?

Next Steps

After implementing your plan:

- How has this approach impacted teaching and learning in your classroom?

- How have your instructional practices shifted, or how do they need to shift in order to make this work?
- How can you free this plan up even more to be more student driven?

REFERENCES

Andrews, J. (2014, June 24). Shipping coffee for adult education. *Centre for Research Innovation and Future Development.* Retrieved from http://thecentreonline.com.au/2014/06/24/shipping-coffee-adult-education/

Australian Institute for Teaching and School Leadership. (AITSL). (2014). *Learning Frontiers.* Retrieved from http://www.aitsl.edu.au/learning-frontiers

Chesser, L. (2013, August 14). 50 Ideas to bring entrepreneurship into the classroom. *Innovation Excellence.* Retrieved from http://www.innovationexcellence.com/blog/2013/08/14/50-ideas-to-bring-entrepreneurship-into-the-classroom/

iLab Capstone Project. (2014). Retrieved on June 5, 2015, from https://sites.google.com/a/dcsdk12.org/mrms-ilab-capstone-project-site/

Loucks, R. (2014). What Is iLab? Retrieved from http://mrms71.weebly.com/when-the-coffee-kicks-in/what-is-ilab

Persichina, M. (2014). Personal Communication.

St. Paul's School. Tagline. (n.d.). Retrieved on June 5, 2015, from St. Paul's School website. Retrieved from http://www.stpauls.qld.edu.au/

Walker, W. (2014, July 23). The happy eating place: How elementary students can run their own business: edutopia. Retrieved from http://www.edutopia.org/blog/happy-eating-student-run-business-whitney-walker

Young Entrepreneurs Academy. (n.d.). Retrieved on June 5, 2015, from http://yeadc.com/

5

Who Owns the Product?

Developing Policies and Procedures

by Homa Tavangar

"Pray for rain, and carry an umbrella."

—Common proverb,
origin unknown

"Product-oriented learning makes the creation and marketing of products the center of the learning experience."

—Zhao (2012, p. 204)

Featured School

University of Massachusetts, Amherst

When University of Massachusetts professor Sut Jhally wanted to find a way to engage his large lecture class as critical thinkers around the exploitation of women's bodies in music videos, he created a mash-up video containing multiple clips. As he found this to be a useful teaching tool, he thought others might too, and offered it to for sale to other educators. Few were actually sold, but shortly afterwards, he received a "Cease and Desist" letter from MTV's lawyers. As it turns out, MTV messed with the wrong guy: Professor Jhally knew that he was entitled to use copyrighted materials under the Doctrine of Fair Use, since his intention was educational. This wrongful accusation meant to scare him (as it does many educators and students) instead spurred him to create the Media Education Foundation (n.d., mediaed.org), which makes and distributes films and other educational materials to inspire critical thinking on mass media. Since 1993, when MTV sent the letter, Jhally has never received any other such threat, even though he's dedicated himself to making many more awareness-raising films, using—and often critiquing—content from numerous sources.

Principles to Consider as You Develop Policies and Procedures

As Professor Jhally's experience shows, knowing key principles around creating and distributing content, as well as some of the right questions to ask along a spectrum from open sharing to tightly controlled ownership, allowed him to stand up for himself, and ultimately helped stimulate a more creative, product-oriented learning environment.

The moment anyone creates a song, book, film, painting, photo, or poem, they automatically own an "All Rights Reserved" copyright. Copyright protects one's creativity against uses they don't consent to. But this might not be restrictive enough. What if someone alters slightly the original work and makes a million dollars? Or, as in the case of Professor Jhally, what if the copyright interpretation is too limiting? Or, if the producers of the music videos he analyzed *wanted* their work to be shared—how would content creators make that known and available? Once you establish a product-oriented learning environment, you can put a framework in place to help address these questions, as well as to help free up creativity.

When you first read the heading of this section on policies and procedures, you might find yourself wanting to run in the opposite direction. After all, you are interested in educating creative, entrepreneurial students that will make their mark on the world—not add new bureaucracy and hoops for them to jump through. We agree. Yet we also expect that many of you will be successful in helping students realize impactful learning. This can lead to product development and expose your school, your students, or you to grey areas of ownership, or even disputes. In other words, if you pray for rain (encourage a product-oriented classroom), then you better carry an umbrella (expect some success and know the issues and protections that you'll need when success comes). In order to both promote a product-oriented classroom and offer guidance on how to protect yourself and your students, we've put together a few suggestions as a roadmap, so that initial policies can be put in place and you can move forward with confidence.

You can think of these considerations like learning grammar when venturing to write. The "rules" simply offer parameters to help avoid confusion and create a common language to build understanding. They should not bog down your creative process. Likewise, some of these considerations add to the literacy or life skills of digital citizens. As you build an understanding of how to use various media and original content in your own products, you aren't only demonstrating knowledge of legal concepts that free your creative process, but also a level of respect for other content creators and for yourself as an active contributor in a creative, participatory culture.

PRINCIPLES FOR DEVELOPING POLICIES AND PROCEDURES FOR A CONSCIENTIOUS PRODUCT-ORIENTED CLASSROOM

- Transform your classroom into an incubator for innovation.
- Embed core values in your policies.
- Establish safety rules.
- Write a business plan.

- Know the basics of intellectual property laws and protections.
- Exercise sound reasoning and judgment when applying fair use.
- Take advantage of Creative Commons copyrights.
- Consider placing your work in the public domain.

Transform Your Classroom Into an Incubator for Innovation

Behind the policy and procedural considerations for a product-oriented learning environment are the many considerations explained throughout this book, as well as a vision and values of how the classroom will be run. This impacts the relationships between students, teacher, the products, and their learning. One such framework that has served successful entrepreneurs, particularly in technology fields, is the incubator. Incubators serve as one-stop shops to help prime the pump for innovation and business development, where one person with a good idea is smart enough that they know they can grow faster and deeper (building solid fundamentals) with the support of a community of experts and peers.

Traditionally, in exchange for a relatively modest fee, or as a prize for a business plan contest, incubators typically provide office space, as well as administrative support, mentoring in strategy and business plan development, and have access to professionals in fields such as finance, marketing, and law. The sheer presence of multiple start-ups in an incubator helps create an atmosphere of idea-sharing, problem solving, creative energy, and collaboration.

As your class increasingly acts like a product-oriented classroom, it can take an identity as an incubator classroom: a safe place to incubate ideas, share and discuss, experiment, test, support each other's ideas, try and try again. Your incubator classroom may use, among its methods, the Design Thinking approach pioneered at Stanford University's Institute of Design "d.school," which is being adopted by a growing number of schools and organizations in building empowering curricula. One such organization, Design for Change, started at the Riverside School in Ahmedabad, India, with partners throughout the world, has identified a simple Design Process summed up in four steps: "Feel, Imagine, Do, and Share". Like the Design Thinking model upon which these four steps are based (depicted below), at the heart and start of this user-centered iterative process is empathy (See Empathy Map and Empathy article by Tavangar, 2014). "Think from your heart" to uncover deep and meaningful needs (both overt and latent) of your audience as you come up with solutions to local or global needs.

Embed Core Values in Your Policies

The Design for Change model serves as an example of identifying not just the processes, but also the core values for your classroom as incubator. These values and identity will in turn help frame questions around policies and procedures that your learning community would like to embrace. While

Figure 5.1 Design-Thinking Process

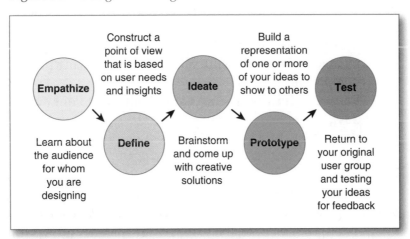

Source: Based on research at dschool.stanford.edu

empathy is a common value embraced by most people, a model like this helps put "bones" on it, to show it translated into disciplined practice. A few ideas from the Makerspace Manifesto include:

- *We share what we make, and help each other make what we share.*
- *It's all right if you fail, as long as you use it as an opportunity to learn and to make something better.*
- *We're not about winners and losers. We're about everyone making things better.*
- *We help one another do better. Be open, inclusive, encouraging and generous in spirit.*
- *We celebrate other Makers—what they make, how they make it and the enthusiasm and passion that drives them.* (Makerspace Playbook, 2013, p. 22, italics added for emphasis)

We were struck by how much emphasis the Manifesto seemed to have on *generosity*—of products, with time, and with one's enthusiasm. Along with an understanding that everyone has the capacity to create, the Manifesto values convey a tremendously supportive environment for trying new things, tinkering, and diversity. As you consider how to craft your classroom policies, try the following reflection exercises:

- Make a list of the core values that your product-oriented, incubator classroom will embody. Post this list in a prominent location.
- Reflect on how these core values will affect your everyday actions.
- Refer back to these core values continuously as you determine policies and procedures.

There are so many values or virtues to choose from (see a sample list of virtues from 52virtues.com), and these are often interrelated. For example, the value of transparency allows for trust, creativity, honesty, and openness to flourish. In countries and companies where transparency is lacking, the tendency to try to get away with dishonest activity soars, quenching innovation. How many admirable inventions or technologies do you hear coming out of the most corrupt countries in the world? Probably close to zero. Aim to nurture a classroom, school, and district that can foster a culture that values rigorous research, information gathering, and transparency—all of which will help lead to the flourishing of innovative ideas.

Stating clearly and practicing your values early and often helps build understanding and depth when facing challenges later on, as dilemmas usually build with success. For example, you may value collaboration, but what does it look like among students in the class with varied interests or even stretching to a wider, global community, when coming up with ideas, research, sourcing, and openly sharing in your learning and creating process? Likewise, the core value of free and open knowledge, where access to information and knowledge is a basic human right, might be adopted. This could translate into allowing unlimited access to the internet or a dramatic reduction in proprietary knowledge and ownership in favor of unlimited access to original content. If your class were to generate income on a product, would you like to be a for-profit (traditional business model) company, a not-for-profit (classified by the U.S. Internal Revenue Service as a 501c3), or a profit-for-purpose venture (see collaborative-consumption.com)? And further, if you make a profit on a product that is invented, would you like to invest the proceeds back into the company, classroom, or school; split the profit among every student; only among those directly identified; or donate all of it to a predetermined charitable organization? Or perhaps your incubator wants to operate based on a barter or sharing economy?

These questions may not be definitively answered, or might take a long time, but they represent some of the hard issues that producers with an authentic audience will face, and that small businesses in incubators might be guided to answer. It is important to withhold judgment that one approach or another is better, either because it seems more charitable, collaborative, or globally oriented. Divergent values need to be taken together and assessed for overall impact in student-driven learning. Additionally, diverse students may weigh values differently: One might be more motivated by profit, and another by social change. This diversity of perspective creates a thriving marketplace and teachers need to be alert to allow their students to determine their own motivations within a context of larger core values, rather than impose their own social or political views. After all, this is modeling the core value of diversity.

Establish Safety Rules

If your product-oriented learning environment includes a makerspace, then policies and procedures will need to consider practical rules for physical safety. The Makerspace Playbook includes a good one-pager (page 15) on Common Makerspace Workshop Rules that you can print out and post prominently wherever tools and supplies might be located. It includes considerations around preparation of the space, clean-up, proper use of tools, proper clothing, and protective gear. Page 66 of the same playbook also includes a Sample Liability Waiver.

Write a Business Plan

A product-oriented learning model calls for a student to convince her teacher to approve the project, and possibly for peers to become partners. This calls for a business plan. While there are thousands of articles online and many books written on the subject, comprised of varying levels of detail, a plan consists of the following basic components:

1. *Company description:* Like an elevator speech, this is a clear snapshot of what you plan to do, and can include your goals, mission, and vision.

2. *Market analysis:* Discuss/analyze the market you are trying to enter, your competitors, and potential customers. Given that background, how will you market your product or service?

3. *Organization and management:* Who will work on this project, why are they suited to this venture, and how will your organization sustain the effort? How do you plan to market the product or service?

4. *Funding and finances:* Develop a cash flow statement so you understand what your real costs are and what they will be in the future. What are your revenue projections and sources of revenue?

Among the excellent sources of business plan know-how to consult, see the U.S. Small Business Administration, a federal government agency, which has some good guidelines on creating your business plan. Sequoia Capital, the legendary Venture Capital fund, translates the parts of a business plan into a format that strives to convey as much information as possible into the fewest words. And the $100 Startup One-Page Business Plan offers a useful worksheet for writing your first serious business plan.

Another helpful tool in business planning is a SWOT analysis. This stands for identifying your venture's Strengths, Weaknesses, Opportunities, and Threats, and can be a good tool for deciding whether or not you actually have a good idea. Though some business planners include SWOT analysis and others don't, we particularly like this tool as an honest self-assessment of a product in the learning process, whether or not you share it with the public you may be pitching for the business.

Note that both the business plan and the SWOT analysis are living documents, meaning that as factors change, the effectiveness or facts of the plan may change too. Check in on the plan every 3 to 6 months to see if you need to make adjustments.

Know the Basics of Intellectual
Property Laws and Protections

One area in which values intersect with policies is around the ownership of ideas and products. These considerations fall under the field of intellectual property.

Intellectual property is simply *the protection of creations of the mind* and at its basic form is divided into three categories:

- Copyrights (©) protect original creations, such as books, video games, movies, characters, and music. They give only the author "the right to copy." You automatically own the copyright on anything you create, but you can register your works for public record with the U.S. Copyright Office. Copyright allows for "fair use" of works, which permits uses without permission that are "beneficial," "transformative," and do not unduly harm the copyright owner (e.g., for educational, news reporting, criticism, or nonprofit purposes).
- Patents: The government grants the legal right to anyone to make or sell an invention that is "new, nonobvious, and useful," generally for 20 years. Once the patent term ends, anyone can re-create or build upon the invention. There is no such thing as an "international copyright" or "international patent" that will automatically protect creators' works throughout the world. Protection against unauthorized use in a particular country depends on the national laws of that country.
- Trademarks (™) and Service Marks can be a word, picture, symbol, or even a sound or smell used to label commercial products or services. It is how consumers can distinguish between different products or services.

Since the founding of the United States, intellectual property has taken on almost sacred proportions, reflecting the Founders' belief that society flourishes when new ideas are allowed to develop and spread. Article I, Section 8 of the U.S. Constitution, signed in 1787, includes the provision, "Congress shall have the power . . . to promote the progress of science and useful arts by securing for limited times to authors and inventors the exclusive right to their respective writings and discoveries." George Washington himself signed into law the first patent act in 1790, and three patents were issued that year. Since then, nearly 8 million patents have been issued, and over 3 million trademarks registered (iCReaTM: Middle School Resource Guide, p. 4). Such provisions don't limit innovation, but rather encourage it, by creating clear ground rules—just like grammar rules don't stifle writing but actually help writing to flourish.

The U.S. Patent and Trademark Office (USPTO), in a quest to spur future innovators in America, created a useful series of elementary, middle, and high school resources around trademarks and patents. Their materials focus on the process of invention and design to come up with creative ways to solve problems and include vignettes of cool, young designers and investors. Students can learn about patents, trademarks, copyrights, and trade secrets by taking a turn at inventing and creating their own trademark designs. The USPTO also has partnered with Girl Scouts of America to create educational materials to demystify the intellectual property protection process. National Geographic's lesson plan on Intellectual Property offers another perspective on these questions, with material for Grades 6–12. The University of Rhode Island's Media Education Lab and nonprofit civil- and digital-rights Electronic Frontier Foundation, offer additional perspectives to help build students' critical thinking and communication skills around this sometimes nuanced issue of copyright education (U.S. Patent and Trademark Office, n.d.-a, n.d.-b).

Knowledge of some of these issues and basic protective steps also demonstrates a level of cognitive complexity few students traditionally gain until after completing university studies and entering law school. By including these considerations in your entrepreneurial learning process you demonstrate how world class learners can leapfrog over traditional, linear curricula.

Exercise Sound Reasoning and
Judgment When Applying Fair Use

For students and teachers interested in creating content (especially digital materials), it is likely you'll also use some content created by others; in fact, it's almost impossible not to. Professor Renee Hobbs's excellent book *Copyright Clarity: How Fair Use Supports Digital Learning* offers clarification of misconceptions common in using materials created by others, and perpetuated by large corporations that stand to gain from others' lawfully using their work. As the book argues, understanding the term *fair use* is vital for liberating digital learning—as we saw in the experience of Professor Jhally in Massachusetts. Knowing about fair use is also important for liberating product-oriented learning. In essence, practicing fair use involves exercising good reasoning and judgment to determine the intention of use and transforming the other party's work to use it for a different purpose than the original.

Professor Hobbs has created a *Code of Best Practices in Fair Use for Media Literacy Education*, which identifies five principles representing acceptable practices for the fair use of copyrighted materials. It states:

Educators can:

1. make copies of newspaper articles, TV shows, and other copyrighted works, and use them and keep them for educational use;

2. create curriculum materials and scholarship with copyrighted materials embedded in them; and

3. share, sell, and distribute curriculum materials with copyrighted materials embedded in them.

Learners can:

1. use copyrighted works in creating new material; and

2. distribute their works digitally if they meet the transformativeness standard [i.e., was the work

used for a different purpose than that of the original, or did it just repeat the work for the same intent and value as the original?] (Hobbs, 2010, p. 73).

Making the judgment on fair use starts with the user of content. To help break down what might seem like an intimidating responsibility, *Copyright Clarity* offers a step-by-step questionnaire to document the fair use reasoning process, asking the following questions:

- What is the purpose of your project?
- Who is the target audience?
- What techniques are you using to attract and hold attention?

To describe the use of copyrighted materials:

- I am using (description of resource used)
- Because (provide the reason)
- Provide a full citation of resource
- Did your use of the work "transform" the material taken from the copyrighted work by using it for a different purpose than that of the original? Explain why your work does not just repeat the intent and value of the original source material.
- Did you use only the amount you needed to accomplish your purpose? Explain why you made your selection. (Hobbs, 2010, pp. 102–103)

Take Advantage of Creative Commons Copyrights

When Science Leadership Academy students built the first-ever flow process bio-diesel "maker," under the guidance of teacher Matt Van Kouwenberg, they considered applying for a patent, but then decided that if used for nonprofit purposes, they would give their machine away. Very soon after making this decision, communities in Ecuador and Guatemala contacted them to use it. This quick adaptation of the student invention was made possible through a Creative Commons license.

Creative Commons (CC), a nonprofit organization, serves as a liberation from traditional copyright restrictions, enabling the sharing and use of creativity and knowledge. The brainchild of Harvard Law School Professor Lawrence Lessig, CC doesn't skirt the law. On the contrary, it offers a framework of free, standardized copyright licenses that encourage sharing and collaboration, switching from the default "all rights reserved" to "some rights reserved." Since its first licenses were released in 2002, CC has become the global standard for sharing, with the number of licensed works growing exponentially every year (e.g., 4.7 million estimated CC licensed works by the end of 2004, 20 million by 2005, 50 million by 2006, 130 million by 2008, 350 million by end of 2009) (Creative Commons History page, 2012).

One creative industry professional, Anil Prasad, shares his experience with the CC framework: "Creative Commons is about treating the entire planet as a single global community, in which media is a shared resource that benefits the human race as a whole. . . . It's about taking your work directly to the people and experiencing and enjoying the unexpected connections that get created" (Mohan, 2013).

With a Creative Commons license, original content might be copied, distributed, edited, remixed, and built upon, all within the boundaries of copyright law. This process still may seem intimidating, cumbersome, or bewildering to those of us untrained in the law, so CC language is packaged in a "three-layer design" comprised of Legal Code, Human Readable (the version that most of us nonlawyers will want to reference), and Machine Readable (formatted so that software systems, search engines, and other kinds of technology can understand). For your reference, Creative Commons provides a "Considerations for licensors and licensees" guide. Licenses follow a spectrum of legal openness and fall under six categories, listed in order from most open to most restrictive.

Creative Commons License Categories

1   Attribution

CC BY

This license lets others distribute, remix, tweak, and build upon your work, even commercially, as long as they credit you for the original creation. This is the most accommodating of licenses offered. Recommended for maximum dissemination and use of licensed materials.

> For example, you might see amateur photographers' photos online, labeled with "This work is licensed under a Creative Commons Attribution 4.0 International License" and wish to use these on your own website. This, and any other use, are allowed, as long as you give credit to the photographer.

2   Attribution-ShareAlike

CC BY-SA

This license lets others remix, tweak, and build upon your work even for commercial purposes, as long as they credit you and license their new creations under the identical terms. This license is often compared to "copyleft" free and open source software licenses. All new works based on yours will carry the same license, so any derivatives will also allow commercial use. This is the license used by Wikipedia, and it is recommended for materials that would benefit from incorporating content from Wikipedia and similarly licensed projects.

For example: The rock band Nine Inch Nails gave away their last album, *The Slip*, by famously licensing it under a creative commons attribution noncommercial share alike license (CC BY-NC-SA). In practice, as they state on their website, this means:

> "we encourage you to
>
> remix it
>
> share it with your friends,
>
> post it on your blog,

(Continued)

(Continued)

play it on your podcast,

give it to strangers,

etc." (Nine Inch Nails, 2008)

Copyright? Or Copyleft?

When students begin to understand their work is automatically copy-righted, they also can realize they have say over this automatic designation, and don't need to follow the default restrictive setting. If they'd like to open up the copyright permission and in essence tell the world that all people are able to use, adapt, copy, or modify their work, they can designate it as "copyleft." In addition to the wide permissions copyleft authorizes, it also means that anyone who modifies the work also needs to make their new creative work available for free as well. Copyleft is automatically a Creative Commons ShareAlike license, but not all ShareAlikes are the same as copyleft, since there are a range of ShareAlike licenses and some contain more provisions. Like ShareAlike, copyleft does contain provisions for attributions (it doesn't ignore all rules), and a few other legal details, but because of its growing use in a range of fields it is a useful term to add to a product-oriented learner's vocabulary. Copyleft is sometimes used interchangeably with the term *openness* in terms of sharing content.

University of Regina Education Technology Professor and advocate of open, collaborative learning, Alec Couros, who blogs at educationaltechnology.ca urges educators to include copyleft in building an understanding of intellectual property issues for digital literacy. As he states regarding all IP (Intellectual Property) terms: "The terms need to be questioned and critiqued, and their history and current emphasis in our laws need to be critically explored" (Couros, 2008). In his "MyBytes . . . Bites!" blog post, he also offers critical questions teachers and students can discuss in assessing dissenting voices on copyright and copyleft, such as noticing the sponsor of a site in order to recognize whose perspective they may represent, considering alternative models of distributing content, and who the beneficiaries of the various models may be (Couros, 2008).

3   Attribution-NoDerivs

CC BY-ND

This license allows for redistribution, commercial and noncommercial, as long as it is passed along unchanged and in whole, with credit to you.

4   Attribution-NonCommercial

CC BY-NC

This license lets others remix, tweak, and build upon your work noncommercially, and although their new works must also acknowledge you and be noncommercial, they don't have to license their derivative works on the same terms.

5   Attribution-NonCommercial-ShareAlike

CC BY-NC-SA

This license lets others remix, tweak, and build upon your work noncommercially, as long as they credit you and license their new creations under the identical terms.

> For example: MIT Open CourseWare is a pioneer in releasing its materials under a CC BY-NC-SA license. According to their website, MIT OCW has over 2,260 courses available freely and openly online for anyone, anywhere to adapt, translate, and redistribute and had reached 175 million individual visitors by 2015 (Massachusetts Institute of Technology, 2015). Thanks to the generous work of early leaders like MIT, the OpenCourseWare concept has now spread to hundreds of universities worldwide.

6   Attribution-NonCommercial-NoDerivs

CC BY-NC-ND

This license is the most restrictive of the six main licenses, only allowing others to download your works and share them with others as long as they credit you, but they can't change them in any way or use them commercially.

Attorney Sara Hawkins (2014) explains these attributions in her blog post "Creative Commons Licenses Explained in Plain English." Since CC has really gained momentum in the last decade, and most teachers received the bulk of their professional training before knowing about them, it's natural to be hesitant to use these classifications for student work. However, navigating the creativecommons.org website, resources for teachers like those from the Center for Teaching Quality and Common Sense Media, misconceptions can begin to be dispelled, so collaborating with and sharing media and other content moves forward confidently.

Consider Placing Your Work in the Public Domain

Depending on how important sharing or the free access to information figures among your class values, you may consider a wide-open policy of "no rights reserved" for the original content created in your class. This is considered to be like gifting in a knowledge economy; in a "gift-culture," social status is determined by an author or creator's contributions to an innovation or product.

A "public domain" designation is one way to capture the idea of unlimited access, but this is extremely difficult based on many jurisdiction's laws. This is one reason the CC0 designation was created, even though it is not included on the spectrum of six CC licensing classifications. From the Creative Commons website:

> CC0 enables scientists, educators, artists and other creators and owners of copyright- or database-protected content to waive those interests in their works and thereby place them as completely as possible in the public domain, so that others may freely build upon, enhance and reuse the works for any purposes without restriction under copyright or database law. In contrast to CC's licenses that allow copyright holders to choose from a range of permissions while retaining their copyright, CC0 empowers yet another choice altogether—the choice to opt out of copyright and database protection, and the exclusive rights automatically granted to creators—the "no rights reserved" alternative to our licenses. (From http://creativecommons.org/about/cc0.)

An increasing number of academic organizations are designating their databases of academic papers, research, and other archives as CC0 to allow an unrestricted access to research and information, and thus the flourishing of ideas. The classic example of knowledge sharing has been around free, open-source software by independent developers. The original Linux and Mozilla Firefox represent some of the better-known examples of free, open-source software. Understanding the motivations behind Mozilla's methods is important for understanding the benefits of digital sharing. In the whitepaper, *Why Mozilla cares about Web Literacy*, the authors state:

We [Mozilla] collaborate on a global basis to ensure everyone can be informed contributors and creators of the web. This act of human collaboration across an open platform we believe to be essential to individual growth and our collective future.

Mozilla helps people develop web literacy: we help them build, not just consume, the technology, media and information that makes up the web. Whether through the thousands of volunteers who write code for Firefox or the growing community that is designing courses for teaching the web, Mozilla strives for an Internet that is:

- Knowable: it's transparent—we can see it and understand it
- Interoperable: it presents opportunity to play and innovate
- Ours: it's open to everyone and we define it (Mozilla, n.d.)

Inherent in this values statement is a vision for those who navigate the Internet to not simply act and be treated as passive users, but also to create and participate on the Web—as true producers. Leadership from organizations like Mozilla can offer an important example of a new way to think about product-oriented learning, with a much wider range of incentives and possibilities than was imagined a generation ago, and a whole new significance to the meaning of sharing.

How to Free Your Work—*Sita Sings the Blues*

The website QuestionCopyright.org describes in its mission statement how, "being on the same side as the audience can have better economic results than monopoly-based distribution." Nina Paley, author and filmmaker of the highly acclaimed and freely distributed animated film *Sita Sings the Blues* exemplifies this ethos by putting her work in

(Continued)

(Continued)

the public domain. In Paley's blog post for the site on "How to Free Your Work" (Paley, 2011), she offers a step-by-step process creators can use to make it as easy as possible for people to share their work, archive it, and receive payment in the form of voluntary contributions or fees for "containers" of work—and her entrepreneurial experience shows that this is a great way to build a bigger audience. *Sita Sings the Blues* was distributed freely to anyone who cared to watch it. As a result, it got an enormous audience for her quality work and made money too. She made the content (the streaming film) free, and the "containers" (hard-copy DVDs, t-shirts, printed materials) not free. Because the film is so excellent, viewers also felt welcomed into a community where they want to "donate" something for having watched the film. Besides the model of the band Nine Inch Nails cited earlier, British blockbuster band Radiohead followed a similar model and author Paolo Coehlo offers his content for free when available digitally. Granted, Radiohead and Coehlo are both internationally adored with millions of fans each, but Nina Paley was not. Each, however, made an important statement about the open sharing of content and ideas and showed the critical principle of the digital age: Building a wide base of supporters and awareness is often a bigger key to success than collecting a set fee for a very limited number of products that might sell.

Strategies for Establishing a Product-Oriented Classroom, School, and District

This chapter has dedicated much space to understanding the various designations and practices for sharing and protecting ideas as well as the vision and values of the learning community that are vital to determining policies and procedures. In practice, here are some steps for creating your own policies and procedures. (Note that the designations of beginning, intermediate, and advanced are fluid—one step may apply equally at a more advanced stage of policy development as at the beginning. Read through all the recommendations here as any of them might apply to your specific circumstances).

Thinking About—Beginning

- *Identify your values.* When you have become informed on the issues in this chapter and throughout this book, discuss as a class what values you will prioritize. This process might take a longer time than you expect and require multiple revisions, as concepts like sharing and collaboration may seem simple at the start, but become more complex once applied to actual products you create. These values also reflect ethical considerations of your student-driven learning. Once identified, policies and procedures should mirror classroom, school, and district values.

- *Build your vocabulary.* The product-oriented student will grow their vocabulary of ownership policies as their experience becomes more complex. Knowing and using terms like attribution, collaboration, incubator, Creative Commons, crowdsourcing, authentic audience, and Intellectual Property will free up producers to spend more time creating, and less time worrying or questioning the value of their work—and you'll be speaking the same language.

- *Create a plan.* The ability of students to elucidate what they want to do, why, and who the audience is, whether creating a technology they plan to sell to the entire world, or making a video that younger classmates might watch to learn a math concept, forms a foundation to building product-oriented learning skills. A simple outline of an intended product can be the first step to creating a business plan, and this can progress in complexity to include projected market share and Return on Investment, depending on the complexity of the project and sophistication of the students.

Implementing—Intermediate

- *Build a bank of resource people.* As an incubator classroom, reach out to parents and other members of the community with expertise in skills business and social entrepreneurs will need. These include IP (intellectual property) lawyers, people who work in manufacturing or technology companies, marketing, design, and branding professionals. Many cities, counties, and universities also have economic development organizations with consultants who work with area entrepreneurs on similar issues and may be very enthusiastic to work with students. Invite them to come in to speak with your class or group about their work. This will allow you to gauge their chemistry with students, to help you determine if you wish to invite them to serve as advisors to your incubator. These resource people also might help facilitate future internships or research projects tied directly to their own work.

- *Learn from the best in the world.* Alan November, author and school advisor, advocated that we consider "who is the best in the world at whatever it is you're teaching?" (A. November, personal interview, August 26, 2014.) For example, we've mentioned Stanford's d.school and IDEO for design-thinking and applying innovative design to any challenge. Or for a Science Olympiad team, look to students in Singapore and learn from them, whether it's following and communicating directly with a group on Twitter, researching resources from their perspective (e.g., using "site:sg" in the search box so search results match what they would get in Singapore, versus simply typing a basic term into the Google search); or gaining know-how from the best global business minds like those at INSEAD or the *Harvard Business Review* by following them on Facebook or diving deeper into their research journals.

- *Have students keep an invention or innovation journal.* As they record their progress, students also document their ownership of the idea. Witnesses from class, particularly the teacher/venture capitalist, can sign pages that document its evolution. Some organizations feel more comfortable having a notary public sign pages, and many schools already have an authorized notary in the building.

- *Invest in teacher development.* For teachers to stand on solid ground around innovation, intellectual property and being able to encourage their students' creativity, professional development in these advanced areas will go far to help students thrive and produce.
- *Don't be afraid of the fine print: Read click-wrap agreements.* Intellectual property concerns at K–12 schools and districts have generally been confined to issues of preventing plagiarism, illegal downloads of music and video content, and privacy violation. In one case turning the tables, four high school students in Virginia and Arizona sued iParadigm, maker of the popular anticheating Turnitin platform, claiming that the company illegally archived students' work without their permission, and that the antiplagiarism system violated educational privacy laws by retaining personal information about them. The judge, however, ruled in favor of iParadigm and dismissed the case, ruling that the "I Agree" contract, known as a click-wrap, was valid, as was the license to keep students' work in their database.

  While one take-away can be that users must read the "I Agree" fine print and opt-out of submitting work on a cloud-based database if they can't stomach this level of sharing work, it's also nearly impossible to enter many websites or applications without first checking the "I Agree" box, putting users in a serious bind. QuestionCopyright's Minute Meme video by Nina Paley should stimulate serious inquiry about checking the agreement box that most Internet users take as a given. You can discuss if your class would like to take a stand on this issue.

Expanding—Advanced

- In the spirit of some business or social impact incubators, create financial infrastructure (raise funds) to incentivize innovation and POL (product-oriented learning). A small investment fund to encourage entrepreneurial activities or social change investments offers a tangible incentive to student innovators. You can look to raise funds to support product design, marketing, experiential travel, or charitable giving and activities from among the mentors to the class and their employers, from area businesses, from community foundations with a hyperlocal focus and other foundations, or even through crowdfunding like Kickstarter.com and Indiegogo.com. Specific grants for makerspaces can be found at makergrants.blogspot.com. For social change projects, having a listing on GlobalGiving.com could serve as a great source of crowdfunding and exposure, while also professionalizing your effort.

- If showing at a competition or public fair you have one year from public display to file a patent (in the United States). If interested in taking a more traditional route to IP protection and you wait more than a year, you lose your right to a patent. If showing your product outside the United States, and protection is important to you, you may want to consult a patent attorney first, as laws vary, and it could be too late to obtain protections once you've shown your product publicly.

- In cooperation with a professional, have students work in teams to draw up a simple contract. This process will force them to plan for detailed steps in the process as well as consider pitfalls along the way and ask hard questions. You can access standard contracts, but applying the template to individual proposals creates an important learning experience.

- Clarify who owns what and expectations from the beginning. As a class, school, or district, it's vital to clearly spell out content ownership; and if any income is to be generated, what would be done with that income? Ideally, students who are producers of content would decide among themselves and their teacher, as a consensual, informed group decision, but in other cases, administrators make these decisions from the top down. One Maryland school district decided they would own the copyright to all student content, even amidst questionable legality (i.e., the creators of content automatically own the copyright, not the school in which the content was made) and to the chagrin of some students and families (Bogle, 2013). When partnerships across locations are involved (i.e., two or more schools or two teachers collaborate to create a study tool app or website that generates income), creating clarity from the outset on ownership and responsibilities is vital in order to maintain a strong partnership.

Overcoming Challenges

- As values are being enunciated, take care to listen to as many student voices as possible and create opportunities for quieter voices to be heard, so they aren't drowned out by louder ones.
- Policies and procedures should reflect both business and social-impact products, not favor one over the other, depending on your personal or community biases.
- Principles of business planning can apply to a nonprofit venture as well as to a for-profit enterprise, and the business plan itself can be a simple, one-page document. It does not need to be long in order to be effective.
- A partial or incomplete understanding of ownership and fair use policy can expose your student-producers to justified or unjustified accusations.
- A commonly accepted, though inaccurate understanding of ownership and fair use policy can limit the types of education projects students are allowed to do, and the extent of media they can lawfully access.
- Knowing your rights and becoming bogged down in legalese are two different things entirely. Taking some time to understand what can be used and reproduced, and other ownership matters will serve as a solid investment in creating a product-oriented mindset, without making legal precautions the focus of learning or the deterrent to creativity.

Why We Want to
Take on the Challenge . . .

A basic knowledge of rights and responsibilities of ownership and content sharing, enunciated simply in policies and
procedures designed in consultation with students, can serve
as an effective tool for cultivating product-oriented learning,
and possibly even help to liberate creativity. Establishing the
atmosphere for product-oriented learning to flourish through
the clear articulation of a vision and values that your group
collectively decides upon reinforces the message that flourishing creativity amidst entrepreneurial thinking is a priority.
Values can reflect principles of sharing, generosity, respect,
excellence, diversity, resilience, responsibility and can be
somewhat fluid to respond to realities of your learning community and its goals. Knowing about effective procedures,
raising funds to invest in developing products or simulating
an incubator environment all may require you to step out
of your comfort zone and pursue professional development
through nontraditional means.

As your class, after-school group, or entire school begins
its product-oriented expedition, consider the spectrum from
tight ownership and control to wide-open sharing.

- Which operating models do you admire most? Why?
- What values would you put in place to reflect your process of creating and learning?
- After half a year with these in place, what would you
  like to change?
- As a group, will you seek unanimity or majority consensus to move ahead with establishing policies and
  procedures?

Asking some of these driving questions can help fill in
procedural gaps while also building confidence that a product-
oriented learning approach is doable—one step at a time.

Activity #1: What Are Your Core Values, Really?

Participants: Teachers, school administrative teams, or district-level educators; then repeat with students

Objective: In this chapter we identified Design Thinking pioneered by the Stanford d.school and the Design for Change model that can serve as examples of identifying not just the processes, but also the core values for your classroom as *incubator*. These values will in turn help frame questions around policies and procedures that your learning community would like to embrace.

The objective in this activity is to ideate—creative, unrestrained brainstorming—the values underpinning your product-oriented classroom, or incubator, then prioritize key values. Use the text in Chapter 6, under "Core Values Embodied in Your Policies" as a guide to get started with ideation.

- List all the values you'd like your "incubator" to embody.
- Prioritize these.
- Repeat the exercise with your students and compare your vision and values to your students.

Materials

- Post-It notes
- Colored markers
- Blank, unlined paper
- Note: You might want to make a physical list that "pops" and can be posted prominently, or you might make an electronic list, then when conferring with students come up with a final list in consultation with them. In this latter case, you won't make a poster until after you've returned to your class and conducted this exercise all over again.

Organization: Groups of four to six

Process: (40 minutes total)

> *Ideation* (10–15 minutes): After re-reading the sections from Chapter 6 on "Vision: Classroom as Incubator" and "Core Values Embodied in Your Policies" write down all the values that you think could help develop your classroom as an incubator classroom.
>
> *Consider and Prioritize* (10 minutes): Have each participant write down their own list of 10 or fewer values they'd like reflected in their classroom, and prioritize these, from the most to least significant. This is a draft, or "first-round" list that is meant to be edited.
>
> *Reflection* (15 minutes): Within your groups share your prioritized lists. Actively listen to opinions that differ from your own. Upon reflection, consider if you would change the order or contents of your list. If there is time and inclination, make a colorful poster to bring back to your class.

Next Steps: Application in the Classroom (Now What?)

Repeat this process with your classroom. Do not show your own Core Values poster to the class until after they have considered, reflected and come up with their own small group consensus on values. Once the students have completed their discussions, show your Core Values list. Would you keep it as is, now that you've heard your students' considerations? How was their thinking process different or similar to your initial experience?

ACTIVITY #2: IS IT FAIR USE?

Participants: Teachers and students

Objective: Walk through some questions presented in Chapter 6 that help product-oriented learners determine if they are using other people's creations fairly during the process of creating your own product.

Materials

- Sticky notes and sheets of plain paper (8 ½ x 11)
- Internet access and digital tools for conducting Web searches

Organization: Have participants organize themselves in groups of two to four.

Process

Determine the product you'll make (5 minutes): You might choose to deliver a TED-style talk about a favorite hobby, city, or idea (e.g., education reform, secrets to happiness, ingredients needed to get an A+ in your class), create an app (learn a foreign language; a better game of Scrabble; how to flawlessly entertain 30 people for dinner), or a time-saving consumer product that can clean your home, drive you to work, or discipline your children. These of course are hypothetical for the purpose of this exercise only, to serve as a starting point for the main lesson of this activity—understanding Fair Use.

Document the fair use reasoning process (15 minutes): Using your hypothetical product you wish to create, complete these questions cited in Chapter 6, with your small groups:

- What is the purpose of your project?
- Who is the target audience?
- What techniques are you using to attract and hold attention?

To describe the use of copyrighted materials:

- I am using (description of resource used)
- Because (provide the reason)
- Provide a full citation of resource

- Did your use of the work "transform" the material taken from the copyrighted work by using it for a different purpose than that of the original? Explain why your work does not just repeat the intent and value of the original source material.
- Did you use only the amount you needed to accomplish your purpose? Explain why you made your selection. (Hobbs, 2010, pp. 102–103)

Determine fair use and any other permissions needed (5 to 15 minutes): Based on rudimentary criteria offered in Chapter 6, as well as additional research your team may conduct, can you make a case for having met fair use standards? What other permissions, documentation, or licensing will be needed to create your product?

Reflection (now what?) (15 minutes): Share with the other groups your process and how you determined fair use and any other copyright issues. Is there agreement across groups with the way you handled it? Does this change the way you'll use outside materials in your own classroom? What are the most important principles you'd like students to take away from this learning?

REFERENCES

Bogle, A. (February 13, 2013). Maryland wants to copyright students' homework. Retrieved from http://www.mhpbooks.com/maryland-wants-to-copyright-students-homework/

Couros, A. (February 13, 2008). My Bytes . . . Bites. Retrieved from http://educationaltechnology.ca/couros/786

Creative Commons. (n.d.-a). About CC0—"No Rights Reserved". Retrieved from https://creativecommons.org/about/cc0

Creative Commons. (n.d.-b). About the Licenses. Retrieved from https://creativecommons.org/licenses

Creative Commons. (n.d.-c). History. Retrieved from https://creativecommons.org/about/history

Hawkins, S. (2014). *Creative commons licenses explained in plain English.* http://sarafhawkins.com/creative-commons-licenses-explained-plain-english/?utm_source=www.inbound.org

Hobbs, R. (2010). *Copyright clarity: How fair use supports digital learning*. Thousand Oaks, CA: Corwin.

Maker Media. (2013, Spring). *Makerspace Playbook, School Edition* (pp. 22–23). Retrieved from http://makered.org/wp-content/uploads/2014/09/Makerspace-Playbook-Feb-2013.pdf

Massachusetts Institute of Technology. (2015). *MIT OpenCourseWare website*. Retrieved from http://ocw.mit.edu/about/

Media Education Foundation. (n.d.). An interview with Sut Jhally. http://www.mediaed.org/wp/about-mef

Mohan, M. (2013, October 14). CC talks with: Innerviews' Anil Prasad—Music Without Borders. Retrieved from http://creativecommons.org/tag/journalism

Mozilla. (n.d.). Webmaker Whitepaper: Why Mozilla cares about web literacy. Retrieved from https://wiki.mozilla.org/Webmaker/Whitepaper

Nine Inch Nails. (2008). The Slip. Retrieved from http://dl.nin.com/theslip/signup

November, A. (2014, August 26). Personal Interview.

Paley, N. (2011, June 24). How to free your work. Retrieved from http://questioncopyright.org/how_to_free_your_work

U.S. Patent and Trademark Office (n.d.-a). iCReaTM: Middle School Resource Guide. http://www.uspto.gov/sites/default/files/kids/icreatm_guide_ms.pdf

U.S. Patent and Trademark Office. (n.d.-b). Kids' pages. Retrieved from http://www.uspto.gov/kids/kids.html

ADDITIONAL RESOURCES

$100 startup: One-page business plan

http://100startup.com/resources/business-plan.pdf

Callan, David. Click Wrap. How click-wrap contracts benefit over shrink-wrap contracts.

http://www.akamarketing.com/click-wrap-shrink-wrap-contracts.html

Camp Invention: An organization working to spur innovation for young people

http://www.campinvention.org/educators

Center for Teaching Quality: Creative Commons resources for classroom teachers

http://www.teachingquality.org/content/blogs/bill-ferriter/creative-commons-resources-classroom-teachers

Collaborative Consumption

http://www.collaborativeconsumption.com/about

Common Sense Media: What is creative commons and why does it matter?

https://www.graphite.org/blog/what-is-creative-commons-and-why-does-it-matter#

Creative Commons: Considerations for licensors and licensees

https://wiki.creativecommons.org/wiki/Considerations_for_licensors_and_licensees

Crowd Funding Kickstarter.com, Indiegogo.com, makergrants.blogspot.com, GlobalGiving.com

Design for Change, started at the Riverside School in Ahmedabad, India

http://www.schoolriverside.com

Design Thinking Approach

http://dschool.stanford.edu/use-our-methods

Educating About Intellectual Property

http://www.educateip.org/index.php/home

Educator's guide for helping to clarify fair use in the classroom

http://www.copyrightfoundation.org/files/userfiles/file/EducatorsGuide.pdf

Electronic Frontier Foundation: Teaching Copyright and Public Domain Frequently Asked Questions

http://www.teachingcopyright.org

http://www.teachingcopyright.org/handout/public-domain-faq

Empathy Map

http://dschool.stanford.edu/wp-content/themes/dschool/method-cards/empathy-map.pdf

Guidelines on Creating Your Business Plan
https://www.sba.gov/writing-business-plan

Makerspace grants can be found at
http://makergrants.blogspot.com

Minute Meme video by Nina Paley. User Agreements.
https://youtu.be/W04LFvH1K8Y

National Geographic: Intellectual Property: Innovation and Invention
http://education.nationalgeographic.com/activity/intellectual-property-innovation-invention

Nonprofit civil- and digital-rights Electronic Frontier Foundation
http://www.teachingcopyright.org

Question Copyright. About QuestionCopyright.org
http://questioncopyright.org/about

Registering a Copyright with the U.S. Copyright Office
http://copyright.gov/fls/sl35.pdf

Sequoia: Writing a Business Plan
http://www.sequoiacap.com/grove/posts/6bzx/writing-a-business-plan

Starting a Nonprofit Organization
https://www.snpo.org/resources/startup.php

Tavangar, Homa. (2014). Empathy: The most important back-to-school supply.
http://www.edutopia.org/blog/empathy-back-to-school-supply-homa-tavangar

United States Patent and Trademark Office: Girl Scouts of America IP Patch Guides
http://www.uspto.gov/kids/guides.html

The University of Rhode Island's Media Education Lab
http://mediaeducationlab.com

Virtues: The Gifts of Character
http://virtuesproject.com/Pdf/EVGPoster.pdf

The Makers' School

Creating a Culture and Environment for Product-Oriented Learning

by Gabriel F. Rshaid

"The second way education alters a society's entrepreneurial talents is by decreasing or increasing the level of entrepreneurial capability, such as self-confidence in individuals, by rewarding or punishing certain behaviors. As a result, the overall level of entrepreneurial qualities is decreased or increased."

—Zhao (2012, p. 95)

Featured School

St. Andrew's Scots School, Buenos Aires, Argentina

Toward the end of the school year, back in 2007, a group of seniors requested a meeting with the principal of St. Andrew's Scots School in Buenos Aires, Argentina. They wanted to express their concern about the school having decided to close a long-standing community service project in the province of Tucumán, in the north of the country, in a region suffering from endemic poverty. The principal patiently explained the rationale for not continuing the project: The region was too far away, there were issues regarding the safety of students, and staff members who had sponsored and chaperoned the trip for many years felt that the school had already done all they could for that community.

The students, however, felt differently. They were emotionally involved with the community in Tucumán, having gone on service-learning trips for most of their high school years, and expressed strongly that they would like to continue sustaining the project on their own. Thinking that they would never show up again, the principal challenged them to come back at the beginning of the next school year and promised to give them the support of the school if they undertook the project by themselves.

Seven years later, this pioneer group of approximately 30 students can look back and reflect proudly on the incredible achievement of having created Minkai.org, an NGO (nongovernmental organization) that has not only continued the community service work originally started by the school but stretched it even further:

- There were more than 200 volunteers recruited.
- Scholarships for the young students at the local school were provided.
- The high school students themselves train teachers at the local schools.
- The Tucumán students' quality of life was thus radically improved.

Due to their admirable efforts and successes, Minkai.org has been featured in local and international media. This story is inspirational simply on the grounds that these entrepreneurial young people cared enough

(Continued)

(Continued)

to give their time and effort to serve others. "Only those who have experienced the happiness of helping others selflessly can understand why 40 young people in Argentina spend their Sundays and holidays traveling thousands of miles to help the inhabitants of a small town called Palominos" (Zolezzi, 2013). However, the real success story is how they undertook a seemingly impossible task as recent high school graduates and succeeded in developing an exemplary project. The road to success was not without its bumps. The students had to recreate and reinvent their mission and vision several times over the years, recruit and train new student graduates over time, evolve from a focus on providing material help to a focus on education, secure funding, and sustain the organization through the inevitably difficult process of any startup. Throughout the process, the students demonstrated exemplary entrepreneurial success.

Looking back, there are, of course, very valuable individual contributions to this collective effort, and it would be unfair to deny the exceptional qualities of many of the students who led and developed the project. But the lesson to be learned lies in understanding what made their success possible, how these students had the confidence, the skills, and the tools to undertake an overwhelmingly difficult task and not only succeed, but find meaning in the process. The factor that stands out most prominently is the unique school culture of St. Andrew's Scots School that equipped these students with the confident mindset they needed to deal with a challenging real life problem and the passion and commitment to tackle it head-on.

PRINCIPLES FOR CREATING A CULTURE AND ENVIRONMENT FOR PRODUCT-ORIENTED LEARNING

Schooling is more than the sum of the parts, and nothing is probably as powerful within education as the school culture, the underlying and sometimes indescribable and undefinable set of collective expectations set by the school leadership. When we look at a painting, it is almost inevitable that we are initially attracted to whatever is presented on the foreground of the picture, and we seldom look at the background. But it is the background that provides the context and that allows for the main focus of the picture to emerge in its true light. This chapter will focus on how to develop a school culture that fosters the learning of the higher-order skills that characterize the entrepreneurship process.

- Take risks and learn from failure.
- Embrace creativity.
- Understand the needs of the project.
- Plan and organize.
- Collaborate.
- Foster an open culture.
- Unlearn and relearn.

Take Risks and Learn From Failure

The students in our story were able to develop a successful social entrepreneurship project through many positive actions because they had the resiliency to be able to learn from their mistakes, backtrack their steps, redo their vision, and come up with new strategies to try to accomplish their objectives. They were able to see beyond the momentary frustration of failed schemes and plans and move from a model that attempted unsuccessfully to provide help with material needs to one that planted the seed for long-term improvement of their communities through education.

Probably the foundational stone of any entrepreneurship attempt is how the people involved can raise their level of self-confidence to attempt an undertaking that, by definition, may not be successful. One of the most popular trending topics in later years in education has to do with how to encourage our students to be risk takers, to understand that failure is part of the learning process, and other similar variations of the same theme. Despite there being a good level of consensus that grit and determination and overcoming failure are extremely valuable assets, very little is done in most schools to consciously nurture those attributes.

An essential element of school culture that provides an adequate background for students to attempt to solve real-life problems, to develop some of the entrepreneurial traits, and look at the world from the viewpoint of opportunity is that we make true on this fashionable premise and that mistakes are not stigmatized, as is still, regretfully, often the case in most school environments.

Embrace Creativity

Through their collective efforts, the students in our project were able to think outside of the box and move away from the cliché of just supplying the community with material help as well as realize that any long-term improvement that had a greater impact would be achieved through the nonconventional method of providing the students in the community with the opportunity to study and then give back in an effort to raise the community and try to solve the endemic poverty issue.

None of this would have been accomplished if they had not had the habit of looking beyond compliance, if they had not asked themselves lots of questions before falling to the temptation of the easiest route, which always consists of following conventional wisdom and doing your best effort even when it is known that it won't be enough. Another dominant element in an entrepreneur culture is, of course, fostering creativity in students. And once again, as we will find with most of the building blocks of the product-driven culture, policymakers, thinkers, and authors pay lip service to the importance of creativity in the school environment, but very little is done to really create instances where creativity is learned by students and subsequently rewarded through assessment.

Long thought to be one of those innate qualities that people either have or don't have, many current authors have demonstrated that creativity is simply another skill that can be learned and grown. Tina Seelig, the executive director of the Stanford Technology Ventures Program, author of the book *inGENIUS: A Crash Course on Creativity*, stated in an interview that "The biggest myth about creativity is that it isn't important and that it can't be learned. In fact, it is one of the most important skills we can master. . . . And these skills can be learned" (Smith, 2012).

Fostering an environment where creativity becomes an integral part of the school culture is a long-term effort that starts from a very early age, when students are naturally creative and uninhibited, and then follows up with the challenge, as school becomes more formalized and falls prey to some of the internally or externally imposed structures, of keeping students healthily creative as they progress over the years.

Understand the Needs of the Project

A key element for the success of the social project we outlined above is that students were permanently attuned to the needs of the community served. Being able to constantly ask themselves what would make a greater impact in the area is what ultimately motivated them to reshape their plans and be more effective.

It is not by coincidence that they were able to come up with ideas that served a specific purpose. Even though it is not considered to be the primary objective, one of the most important roles of the schooling experience for children of all ages is to develop the critical ability to ask questions, to not take anything for granted, to develop critical thinking insights that allow them to see beyond the superficial level of reality that we are all exposed to in a world that is presenting us with increasingly overwhelming stimuli.

Once again, much has been written about the need to focus more on the questions and the answers, to invert the center of gravity of the instructional process so that students spend more time pondering the problem and analyzing its context and its implications than actually solving it.

In his book, *The Myths of Innovation,* author Scott Berkun relates one of the many Einstein stories that, even if they are not true, are worth learning from: "Einstein once said, 'If I had 20 days to solve a problem, I would take 19 days to define it,' a gem of insight lost in the glory of what he achieved on that 20th day" (Berkun, 2010, p. 126).

Having surrendered to our traditional structures, schooling has pretty much relied on the conventional adult-centric sequence where it is the role of the teacher to lay out the problems and for students to solve them. Nothing prevents us, from the day students enter school in kindergarten all the way until they graduate, to gradually train them not only to solve problems, but also to ask good questions and to try to come up themselves with the problems that need resolving.

Plan and Organize

Another secret to Minkai's success is that students were aware from the very onset that unless they provided some structure and formal planning to their endeavor, they had absolutely no chance to achieve their objectives. If they were able to sustain their initiative over the years, it is because they invested a significant amount of time and effort in planning and then assessing whether they had accomplished their goals.

Like with many of the other elements that we have outlined above, planning and organizing are one of the many important aspects of an entrepreneurial education that are often neglected by most school systems. Project development, organizing and planning, setting deadlines, goals, and objectives, may sound like a very business-oriented framework and therefore relegated to some specific subjects in high school, but project management skills in the world of limitless opportunities and lifelong learning are capacities that all students need to develop in order to at least be able to plan their own personal and professional development. Schools usually do a good job of preparing students to be patronized by an employer or organization, who create a self-serving culture to which individuals adapt (and sometimes lose their identity in the process), but we are not preparing our students equally well for a world that requires independent assessment and planning so that they can find their niche in an increasingly globalized and overconnected world.

Collaborate

Another distinctive feature of the process that the students underwent is how they were able to develop collective reflexes to be able to effectively collaborate amidst a very challenging environment and a technically complex set of challenges that they had to face.

Probably the greatest anachronism in school systems has to do with the insistent systemic focus on individual achievement. So much so that most of our assessment methods have been tailored to recognizing and evaluating individual performance.

It is well known, however, that the moment our students step out from the formal learning environment, they will be required to work collaboratively and often with their colleagues and peers from very remote locations, taking advantage of technological tools that have effectively obliterated distances.

The collaborative aspect of real-life product creation is absolutely essential and key to the success of any entrepreneurial undertaking. Being able to function effectively as part of the team, so that the sum of individual contributions generates aggregate value, is almost a requirement for any real-life work project. The same could be said about the school environment. Collaboration should be the norm and not the exception, and again, from the beginning of their school lives, students should be encouraged and trained to work collaboratively with a sense of purpose and being aware of their role and contribution to the team.

Foster an Open Culture

An integral part of the growth process of the student project referenced in the story was related to their ability to critique each other, and to seek input from different collaborators and volunteers in the project so as to eventually reassess their actions and plans. Being able to benefit from other people's ideas is a very important part of the creation and development process for any project and should not happen serendipitously, but rather as a consequence of intentional actions in the design of curriculum and in the planned instances of students' development in their school years. Reflecting, critiquing, soliciting, and learning from input, providing suggestions, and many other variations of the same process all constitute very valuable skills that students should be bred into regardless of subject matter and age level. When looking at the prevailing pedagogy, once more we find that these processes are, at best, implicit in the development of some school activities, but very seldom addressed and focused to add to the prevailing school culture.

Unlearn and Relearn

Finally, one of the defining traits of the social entrepreneurship project that we have portrayed as an example is these students' ability to unlearn and relearn. Throughout various instances in the development of their project, they had to shift gears, assess what they had accomplished against their objectives, and go through a soul-searching process that entailed partially undoing their previous work in order to adopt a different strategy. The whole unlearning and relearning process has become one of the many clichés that abound in educational jargon, but it nonetheless points to the entrepreneurial mindset and constitutes one of the most challenging aspects of redefining schooling to suit a new knowledge paradigm. In effect, within an intrinsically dynamic environment where change is the only thing we can take for granted, learners need to be able to shed off their preconceived notions about solving a problem or ways in which to tackle the development of a project, and be creative and open-minded about different ways and new possibilities that may very well entail unlearning the previously carefully contrived methods.

As with the previous principles, schools are not particularly good at fomenting a mindset that is open to unlearning and relearning. In fact, the very act of unlearning is almost antithetical to school, and teachers find it hard to relinquish the formerly tried and sure ways that they have learned in the past. "It has always been done like that" is almost a mantra in school culture, and not infrequently, many of the pedagogical methods as well as contents and skills that form part of the instructional process go unchallenged and unquestioned forever. A school setting that is more conducive to the development of skills associated with entrepreneurship would also need to develop a culture whereby it is socially accepted that new methods are tried, that there are no sacred cows either in terms of contents or methods or techniques.

STRATEGIES FOR CREATING A PRODUCT-ORIENTED SCHOOL CULTURE

It is time then to try to formulate some specific suggestions as to how policymakers, administrators, and teachers at the classroom level can plant the seeds for the creation and growth of a culture that is fertile to the development of entrepreneurial capabilities. If we always include a disclaimer that these recommendations are never conceived as infallible or fixed kitchen recipes, in this particular section when dealing with how to establish culture, it is even more important to stress that this is not a linear process and that the ideas that ensue may or may not be entirely applicable to each school's or district's particular set of challenges. But, at the same time, we are equally confident that the underlying principles that support each of them will, if not directly translatable universally to every classroom, stimulate thinking for practitioners to build upon them in their own particular context.

In the Classroom

Treat Assessment Instruments as Products

One simple measure to foster an environment that is conducive to product-oriented learning is to ensure that assessment instruments are treated as products themselves, that is, that students are allowed to improve what they have submitted in successive instances, so as to gradually perfect their work.

We should be aware that this very simple change in mindset is quite countercultural to generations of teachers.

Permitting students to successively improve their assignments it directly linked to the idea of risk-taking and learning from failure. In the prevailing model where students have to beg for retests, it is hard to blame them for being compliant, studying to the test, and being absolutely discouraged when they make mistakes, which for the purposes of assessment, are truly irreparable. It is not in vain that the ancestral battlecry of students in the instructional process is, "Will this be on the test?"

Implicit in this attempt to foster a culture of innovation and risk-taking is the downgrading of the importance of grades (pun intended!). The world abounds with stories of very successful entrepreneurs and other creative individuals who did not conform to the academic model and did poorly in school, and were barely able to hold onto their self-esteem, only to blossom when they were freed of the constraints of a formal learning environment. A system of assessment that is less restrictive, and this is applicable universally from kindergarten onwards, leads to a renewed culture that values the product and honors the iterative trial-and-error process that is intrinsic to creation.

Do Away With Averages

An even more radical suggestion is to entirely do away with the mother of all grading instruments, the venerable average, and its close more sophisticated relative, the weighted average, tools that teachers have forever used to measure academic achievement. The basic problem with averages is that they are clearly not oriented to good products, since they take into account the intermediate stages in the learning and development process, which inevitably include failed steps, mistakes, redesigns, and feedback that propitiate better learning.

This is a very concrete step that helps to create a culture favorable to product-oriented learning and entrepreneurship: Instead of averages, if numeric grades are needed, teachers can arrive at those grades by judging the final product and the progress made by students without relying on the retroactive judgment of the process.

Implement an Assessment Process
That Includes Peer Reviewing and Critiquing

We have already seen that one of the stronger elements of the entrepreneurial culture is related to how members of the team can provide valuable input about the development process and that it not only impacts positively the project itself, but also gives team members who are actively engaged in supplying the feedback an opportunity to learn more in ways that will be reflected on their own active role in working on their products and projects.

Even if it entails somewhat relinquishing control of the assessment process, developing a protocol that incorporates peer review and critiquing is undoubtedly another needed way to reform assessment that favors a new mindset where students take responsibility for helping their peers in the learning process and improving the quality of their projects and products. This can be done from a very early age, at a level that allows for the developmental stage of students at that age, so as to gradually help them acquire the habit of reflecting and so that providing objective and constructive feedback becomes second nature, an indivisible part of the learning process.

Train Students in Self-Assessment

Self-assessment has emerged to become a major player in the lifelong learning process. In order to evaluate our own learning and, even more importantly, what else we need to learn, being aware of how much we have learned and whether we have mastered the necessary concepts to continue the development of our project or the solving of or problem becomes an essential skill. Like with any skill, students need to be trained in the very difficult art of being objective about oneself, for the sake of improving the quality of our product. It is an important trait for any entrepreneur to be able to detach herself or himself from any subjective emotional link with what he or she is doing and be able to self-administer a reality check on how the process is going and chances of success.

In the School

Develop Interdisciplinary Projects

The solving of problems in real life is a complex and multidimensional endeavor that automatically integrates many subject matters, as well as requiring very different skills. Even within existing curricula and constraints and without having to reform any of the existing school structures, teachers can partner and develop interdisciplinary projects that are based on real-life issues.

Developing such problems entails that school leaders allow teachers to stray away from the limits of their subject matters and provide spaces for shared planning, follow-up, and assessment of these projects. In this respect, it is important to lift off some of the usual constraints (scheduling, giving teachers prep time, having time for professional development once a week) so that expectations regarding teachers getting together to develop and implement such projects are realistic.

Pose Open-Ended Problems—Encourage Creativity

A culture that fosters creative entrepreneurs will train their students by exposing them to assignments and assessments that not always feature a right or wrong answer, but rather require that they themselves are able to evaluate the effectiveness of the answer provided or the solution produced.

Closely related to this is the intention of developing a culture where students are encouraged to be creative. A simple step toward achieving this consists in including within assessment instruments questions where students are not just rewarded for getting the right answer but for supplying as many plausible answers as possible, thus explicitly calling them to open up the possibilities, and gradually developing the habit of divergent thinking, a precursor to creativity.

School leaders can set the tone by explicitly challenging teachers to include such open-ended questions regularly in assignments, and even reporting progress on the attainment of creativity skills by students to parents. In the same way that schools report grades, information on how well students are mastering creativity can help raise the community's level of awareness as to the importance of creating a propitious climate for the development of entrepreneurial skills.

Ask the Right Questions

One of the defining traits of the entrepreneurial spirit is being able to discover needs and ask the right questions, this process being often even more important than creating and developing a product or a solution. The teaching and learning process can create a culture where students are rewarded for being inquisitive, critical, curious, and challenging assumptions. This can take many simple forms that teachers would come up with themselves within their subject matter and grade level, such as providing students with the answers and asking them to create the questions, having students design experiments in science, having a beginning of unit session where students ask themselves what it is that they need to learn or to solve a problem, and in general, any action that strays away from the ages old model where the teacher supplies the question and students the answer.

Provide Students With Choice

We have devoted a whole chapter in Book 1 of this series, *Personalized Education for Autonomous Learning and Student-Driven Curriculum*, to how students should have a voice and say in developing curriculum, as well as take ownership in their own learning, as a way to lead them gently from a very early age in assuming responsibility for their lifelong learning process.

From providing options and topics within a subject to a schoolwide system that allows multiple pathways for graduation, giving students an explicit role in their learning experience is undoubtedly a strong component of any culture that fosters the development of entrepreneurial skills.

Plan

One of the many skills that are thought to be implicit in the schooling process, instances can be included where teachers have students learning what is involved and experiencing firsthand the difficulties involved in planning a project. Fomenting this aspect of the culture simply requires that, as an initial stage in most assignments done in the regular school process, a plan be developed and pre-approved after consultation with the teacher before actually setting out to do the assignment itself. This planning stage can easily be adapted to the grade level and subject matter and built upon in successive years in school.

Create Subjects That Are Eminently Product Oriented

Without the need to engage in major systemic reform, schools can create year or semester long subjects where students are required, as the main objective of the subject, to develop a project or solve a problem of their choice. It must be stressed that the adults may very well facilitate the process and ensure that some of the skills and contents are acquired in it, but it must be the students themselves who would choose what to solve or what to do. These "workshop" subjects are able to reach across subject matters and, since they are based on a project or problem, they are automatically going to be assessed in a way that breaks apart from the traditional sit-down written test. Having several of these instances throughout the curriculum over the years is a direct way to add to the development of a product-oriented culture.

In the School System

Plan School Activities That
Engage the Local or Global Community

Another way to gradually bridge the gap between the usually sterile environment of school and outside reality is to incorporate, within curricular work that is done at school, regular interactions with the outside community. Some possible ways of doing this include the following:

- Bring in industry experts to help in the evaluation and assessment of projects done by students.
- Similarly, ask parents or community members to act as mentors to groups of students developing projects so as to advise them and hopefully, in the process, expose them to some of the real-life processes that are involved in entrepreneurship.
- Have students evaluate and come up with issues to be resolved that are directly related to needs within the local community, so that they go through the process of understanding needs, and matching their proposed solutions to what can make a real impact.

These processes are not exclusive of the high school setting, and in general, everybody loves to interact with small children and help them in their learning process, especially if there are strong community links.

Sponsor Contests and Economic Stimuli

A great way to foster the development of an entrepreneurial mindset is to have periodic instances, which may be districtwide, where students are challenged to come up with creative and innovative solutions and are rewarded either through conventional awards and the showcasing of their work, or even more interestingly, to the financing of the projects that are formulated in order to solve a real-life problem. These contests are invariably very attractive to students, who rise up to the occasion and usually devote many more hours to the development of these projects than if they are just restricted to the academic environment, thus clearly showing us that they crave for opportunities to engage in meaningful work.

Establish Projects as Graduation Requirements

In many school systems all over the world, graduation exit requirements are often related to standardized tests and passing exams. However, it would be much more important, instead of having to comply with the universal set of standards on a given day, if students are required to develop an extensive real life interdisciplinary project and build it, test it, and roll it out in real life as a graduation requirement.

In the same way that students unconsciously finely hone their test taking skills because the prevailing culture in most schools is related to written tests, if students were aware all throughout their schooling that there are hefty expectations regarding their ability to produce collaboratively a project at the end of the cycle they would undoubtedly, in the intuitive way that children have to rising up to what is expected of them, fine tune their capabilities to produce these projects, thus helping greatly in providing for a culture that is conducive to an entrepreneurial spirit.

ACTIVITY #1: INCORPORATE CREATIVITY IN YOUR ASSIGNMENTS AND ASSESSMENTS

Participants: Teachers, administrators, curriculum coordinators

Objective: Creativity is one of the fundamental skills students need to thrive in the 21st century. Developing creativity skills is a fundamental marker for future entrepreneurs, who must develop creative solutions to problems. The objective of this activity is to take existing classroom assignments and modify them so that they function to develop the skill of creativity.

Materials: Sample classroom assignments from participants' own practice. Alternatively, the workshop leader can furnish standard assignments and assessments.

Process

Most assignments are designed in a way that students have to furnish right or wrong answers. During this activity, take assignments that are currently being used within the classroom practice and reformulate the questions or the assignments themselves. Here are some examples:

- Redesign questions to be as open-ended as possible; questions that elicit several correct answers.
- Design questions challenging students to supply as many *plausible* answers as possible.
- Ask students to create something: a problem, a hypothetical scenario, a lab experiment. The objective, in order to stimulate the learning of creativity, is for students to develop the project or question themselves.
- Include a problem or question to be solved and challenge students to find an alternative question or answer to the one supplied. This can also be extended to, for example, something that has really happened as in "How would history have been different if a certain event had not happened or had transpired differently?" and so on.
- Supply answers, asking students to develop a number of questions that would lead to those answers.

The process involves analyzing the current assignments and reworking them to require more creativity on the part of students.

Reflection

- How might you use what you have learned from this exercise when designing future assignments?

- Challenge yourself to come up with a strategy to incorporate creativity in all of your assignments and assessment materials.
- (If applicable) reflect on why you have often reverted to asking right or wrong answer questions in the past. Do you see that changing in the future? If so, why and how?

ACTIVITY #2: THE BLACK BOX

Participants: Educators, working in groups

Objectives

- To foster the development of an inquiry-based mindset, one that can analyze data objectively and process them in a way that is conducive to product development.
- To take into account the limitations of any process, evaluate the uncertainties, possible errors, gain a measure of how answers can be arrived at through estimations
- To foster ingenuity and creativity by posing an open-ended problem with no definite answer
- Develop the entrepreneurial mindset by not supplying all that is needed to solve the problem

Materials

- One "black box" per group wrapped in a covering that prevents participants from seeing what is inside.
- The contents should be something that will make the activity interesting for those who are trying to guess what is inside. For example, include

  o A metallic object and pad on one side of the box so that when the box is shaken, the sound is muffled on one side
  o Small pieces of paper, or any other indistinguishable object(s)
  o Something that can roll, such as a marble
  o Anything that can allow students to make inferences when moving the box around

Process

- Allocate one box (or container) per group.
- Ask the group to make observations; participants can move the box around and shake it, but not open it.
- Ask the group to formulate a series of conclusions based on their observations.
- Ask the group to guess what is inside.
- At the end of the activity, participants will not be allowed to open their boxes. They will be asked to live with uncertainty.

Participants will feel a persistent urge to open the box, but part of the lesson is that, on some occasions, the limited information that we have is what constitutes the best approximation to the truth. In the creative design process, entrepreneurs often have access to only partial information. In many cases, decisions have to be made based on best estimates rather than a complete understanding of facts.

Reflection

- Ask participants to reflect on the traditional teacher-directed instructional model that does not lend itself well to the fostering of the entrepreneurial mindset and the development of skills and creativity and the ability to innovate.
- How does it feel to not know what is inside the box? What coping mechanisms can you draw on to address those feelings?
- As a teacher, how might you handle student expectations in terms of their need for the teacher to give them a definite answer?
- Reflect on the skill of estimation. If you don't have access to a definitive answer, how can estimation help you come up with a solution for creating a product or solving a problem?
- Reflect on the skills of observation, inference, deduction, analysis, and interpretation. How can these skills

help you when crucial information is missing? How can developing these skills give you the confidence you need to rely on your own interpretations and move forward with a plan?

Next Steps

Design future assignments to incorporate the inquiry-based process.

ACTIVITY #3: DEVELOPING SKILLS IN PRODUCT CREATION

Participants: Educators

Objective: The process of designing and creating a product is a messy one; one that is equal parts inspiration and systematization (not to mention perspiration!). While no one can come up with a detailed, step-by-step, fail-safe process for developing a successful product, there are skills that can be developed that will help along the way. The objective of this activity is to model the development of a mock-product in order to understand the procedure, protocol, and skills needed to design, revise, and redesign a viable product.

Materials

- Sketching materials—paper and pencil
- Participants should have access to a wide variety of different materials that they can use in various ways and that does not stifle the creative process by narrowly channeling the design by virtue of the materials available.
- A well-defined assessment protocol for critiquing and analyzing the designs. The protocol may involve:
  - Writing observations
  - Listing strengths and weaknesses
  - Offering suggestions for product improvement

Process

Preliminary Design

- Each group will sketch at least two preliminary diagrams for a product.
- Each group will decide which materials are needed and their quantities.
- Each group will provide a short written description of their products.

First Review

- Pair each group with another group.
- One group will present, the other will critique and analyze based on the assessment protocol provided.

Choose a design. Based on feedback from the external review and your groups' own assessment, choose one of the preliminary designs to use going forward.

Design Phase

- Refine the preliminary design based on the feedback received.
- Come up with an enhanced sketch or prototype for the product.
- Draft an enhanced written description of the product.

Second Review

- Each group presents a more detailed description or prototype for the other groups.
- The previously assigned review group will provide more focused feedback based on the protocol. (If this activity is conducted over time and online, there is the option of including industry experts or outside participants to participate in the second review.)

Reflection

- What is the role of the "teacher" in this activity? Does this role mirror your own classroom practice? Why or why not?
- What skills are required to complete the activity (for example: objectivity, openness to criticism, curiosity, sharing ideas, revision)? How do these skills incorporate the entrepreneurial mindset? How are these skills transferable to other fields and activities?
- Reflect on the creative process. Is it linear? Why or why not?
- The activity requires that participants design, assess, and redesign. How can this process be transferred to traditional classroom assignments? Do you allow your students to revise their work after it has been assessed? Do you routinely incorporate peer review and self-assessment in your classroom protocols? Do you grade the final product students produce, or each step in the process?
- What kind of feedback was most helpful to you in this activity? How does that relate to the types of feedback you routinely offer your students? How might you revise your assessment and feedback protocols on future assignments to better serve the needs of your students?

REFERENCES

Berkun, S. (2010). *The myths of innovation.* North Sebastopol, Canada: O'Reilly Media.

El trabajo solidario de la Asociación Minkai. (2013). ArInfo. http://www.arinfo.com.ar/notix/noticia/03741_el-trabajo-solidario-de-la-asociacin-minkai.htm.

"Minkai Trabajo Solidario." (2012). Retrieved from https://www.youtube.com/user/EquipoMInkai.

Smith, N. (2012). Who says creativity can't be learned? *Business News Daily.* Retrieved from http://www.businessnewsdaily.com/2471-creativity-innovation-learned.html.

Zhao, Yong (2012). *World class learners: Educating creative and entrepreneurial students.* Thousand Oaks, CA: Corwin.

Zolezzi, C. (2013). Minkai, jóvenes unidos por el sueño de enseñar en Tucumán. *La Nacion.* Retrieved from http://www.lanacion.com.ar/1643701-minkai-jovenes-unidos-por-el-sueno-de-ensenar-en-tucuman.

Index

Note: In page references, f indicates figures and t indicates tables.

A SAGE Publishing Company

Helping educators make the greatest impact

CORWIN HAS ONE MISSION: to enhance education through intentional professional learning.

We build long-term relationships with our authors, educators, clients, and associations who partner with us to develop and continuously improve the best evidence-based practices that establish and support lifelong learning.